T0032074

The Ultimate
St. Louis Cardinals
Time Machine Book

THE ULTIMATE
ST. LOUIS CARDINALS
TIME MACHINE BOOK

MARTIN GITLIN

LYONS
PRESS

Essex, Connecticut

An imprint of Globe Pequot, the trade division of
The Rowman & Littlefield Publishing Group, Inc.
4501 Forbes Blvd., Ste. 200
Lanham, MD 20706
www.rowman.com

Distributed by NATIONAL BOOK NETWORK

Copyright © 2023 Martin Gitlin

All rights reserved. No part of this book may be reproduced in any form or by any electronic or mechanical means, including information storage and retrieval systems, without written permission from the publisher, except by a reviewer who may quote passages in a review.

British Library Cataloguing in Publication Information available

Library of Congress Cataloging-in-Publication Data

Names: Gitlin, Marty author.
Title: The ultimate St. Louis Cardinals time machine book / Martin Gitlin.
Description: Essex, Connecticut : Lyons Press, [2023] | Includes bibliographical references. | Summary: "The Ultimate St. Louis Cardinals Time Machine presents a timeline format that not only includes the Cardinals' greatest moments, such as their eleven World Series titles, but also such notable Cardinal achievements as Rogers Hornsby's two batting triple crowns, Dizzy Dean's 30-win season in 1934, Stan Musial's 17 MLB and 29 NL records, Bob Gibson's 1.12 earned run average (ERA) in 1968, Whitey Herzog's Whiteyball, Mark McGwire's single season home run record, and the 2011 championship team's unprecedented comebacks. The Cardinals have won 105 or more games in four seasons and won 100 or more nine times. Cardinals players have won 20 league MVPs, four batting Triple Crowns, and three Cy Young Awards. All these highlights and more comprise this essential book for all fans of the national pastime" —Provided by publisher.
Identifiers: LCCN 2022056644 (print) | LCCN 2022056645 (ebook) | ISBN 9781493067077 (paperback) | ISBN 9781493075508 (epub)
Subjects: LCSH: St. Louis Cardinals (Baseball team)--History.
Classification: LCC GV875.S3 G57 2023 (print) | LCC GV875.S3 (ebook) | DDC 796.357/640977866--dc23/eng/20221212
LC record available at https://lccn.loc.gov/2022056644
LC ebook record available at https://lccn.loc.gov/2022056645

∞™ The paper used in this publication meets the minimum requirements of American National Standard for Information Sciences—Permanence of Paper for Printed Library Materials, ANSI/NISO Z39.48-1992.

CONTENTS

INTRODUCTION

THE DEPTH OF BASEBALL KNOWLEDGE AMONG CHILDREN IN THE 1960S and 1970s rarely extended beyond the clubs they embraced as fans. There was no cable television on which to watch nightly highlights from parks around the country. The media covered the sport greatly from local angles. National broadcasts were limited to the Saturday Game of the Week. Adults sometimes gleaned information from publications such as *Baseball Digest* and the *Sporting News*. But kids gathered data only about the teams in their cities for which they rooted. And their fandom often blinded them from realistic appraisals.

Such was my affliction growing up on the east side of Cleveland. It was all Indians all the time. I grew increasingly appreciative of the great players of the era. But most wore the uniforms of American League rivals. Interleague play was merely a twinkle in Bud Selig's eye. I became aware of those in the Senior Circuit. Willie Mays. Sandy Koufax. Hank Aaron. Willie McCovey. Bob Gibson. But I knew little about them. Nor did I care to know. If they didn't play the Indians, they were of little interest to me.

What I did understand, however, was that my lowly Tribe was doing something wrong. Their annual descent into either mediocrity or ineptitude forced me to realize the inequalities between my beloved franchise and the successful clubs in the sport. And on top of that list, one that I noted jealously in my mind, were the St. Louis Cardinals. *They* were doing something right.

A quick glance at the standings provided a daily reminder of their greatness. A more thorough knowledge of baseball later in life resulted in a stronger grasp of their balance on the field, continuity in ownership, and shrewdness in the front office that resulted in dominance during that era—and well before. Heck, the Cardinals never lost more than eighty-nine games from 1917 through 1974. They were sometimes average. But they were never lousy.

Their periods of superiority have been pronounced. The champions of the late 1920s. The Gashouse Gang featuring Dizzy Dean that followed. The war-year World Series winners of Enos "Country" Slaughter and Stan Musial. The perennial 1960s title-holders led by such legends as Lou Brock. Orlando Cepeda and Gibson. The stolen-base kings of the 1980s driven by Ozzie Smith and Willie McGee that snagged crowns without power. And the seemingly annual playoff participants throughout the twenty-first century guided by Tony La Russa and Mike Matheny, the latest into 2018 of a long line of St. Louis managers whose extended stays resulted in stability and success.

That sustained brilliance offers welcome challenges to any chronicler of franchise history. One cannot focus solely on the clubs that earned titles for the Cardinals have hoisted eleven World Series championship banners and played in nineteen Fall Classics. That provided this author an opportunity to not only write about those kings of baseball, but also the personalities and motivations of the men who graced their uniforms or worked behind the scenes to make it all happen, including owners Sam Breadon, who purchased the team for a measly $2,000 in 1917 and sold it for $3 million thirty years later, and the legendary beer baron Gussie Busch, who cycled through one general manager after another but maintained continuity in the manager's office and on the field to rule over six pennant and three World Series winners.

It has been offered that St. Louis boasts the most passionate and sophisticated baseball fans in the land. Such claims will always fall under the category of opinion, but it must be cited that the Cardinals have ranked in the top half in National League attendance every season (aside from the 2020 COVID anomaly) but one from 1981 through 2021. One can argue that the lack of an NBA franchise and the loss of the NFL Rams to Los Angeles left the baseball team as the only show in town aside from the NHL Blues. But the counter is that the Cardinals drew wonderfully when St. Louis rooted for fine football teams and the highly competitive NBA Hawks earned annual playoff berths in the 1950s and 1960s.

So, what the heck. Here is to the best baseball fans in America. To paraphrase a quite applicable and famous Anheuser-Busch marketing jingle—this book's for you. Enjoy.

CHAPTER ONE

Go West, Young Men

THE CIVIL WAR AND ITS HORRORS REMAINED FRESH IN THE MINDS OF millions when the newfangled sport of baseball took hold in the major cities and surrounding areas of the eastern United States. Young men embraced the game. New teams popped up everywhere. But the disparity in talent varied greatly.

Among the punching bags of the era were the Washington Nationals. They had grown weary and frustrated over the frequent poundings delivered by dominant clubs from the areas in and around New York City. So, they sought softer competition in the Midwest.

The Nationals succeeded beyond their wildest dreams in racking up victories and massaging their egos. They battered teams with little baseball experience in Ohio, Kentucky, Indiana, and Illinois before taking their traveling show to Missouri. Relative newcomers to the game in St. Louis eagerly awaited their arrival.

They might have questioned that enthusiasm after battling the Nationals. Though some in the growing town gaining a reputation as the Gateway to the West had begun to play the game, they certainly did not do so at nearly the same level as the visitors from the nation's capital. St. Louis housed just two teams before the war—the first game between the two has been traced back to July 9, 1860. The lack of growth in the sport resulted in predictable domination by the Nationals, who clobbered the Unions—the best bunch the area could muster—by the embarrassing score of 123–26. The beasts from the east had destroyed other teams along their march west by large margins.

Included was a 53–10 walloping of a Cincinnati Red Stockings club considered the most powerful of the Midwest.

Connecticut contractor Jere Frain had given birth to baseball in St. Louis in the early 1850s. The former player with the Charter Oak team in Hartford who felt a love for the new game discovered that the craze had not yet reached eastern Missouri. So, he began to recruit players willing to learn the sport. Frain laid out a diamond in Lafayette Park and taught all those interested. As the Civil War raged on several amateur clubs formed, including the Red Stockings, Atlantics, Empires, and Unions.

The shellacking by the Nationals served to strengthen a passion for baseball in St. Louis and motivate its players to hone their skills. The sport had gained enough traction in America to warrant in 1871 the formation of the National Association, which featured franchises in such Illinois cities as Chicago and Rockford, as well as Cleveland and Fort Wayne. But baseball in those Midwest towns lagged. Most of its teams languished in the standings. The Great Chicago Fire destroyed the sport in that town, and by 1873 none of those clubs existed. A year later, only the Chicago White Stockings remained among teams west of Philadelphia.

That is when St. Louis businessman and entrepreneur James R. Lucas stepped in. He had by 1874 raised $10,000 by selling stock at $50 per share to land a team in the National Association called the Brown Stockings, which played at North Grand Avenue Field, future site of Sportsman's Park and Busch Stadium. Lucas understood quite well that competing only with talent from his town could not suffice. So, he used his wealth to lure premier players from the East.

Among them was Lip Pike, the son of a Brooklyn haberdasher who gained historical notoriety as one of the first Jewish baseball stars. The speedy outfielder and middle infielder led St. Louis in batting average (.346), runs batted in, and stolen bases. Legend claimed that Pike was so fast that he once outraced a horse in a 100-yard dash—though it must be admitted that the equine did not break into a full gallop until his human competitor had sprinted seventy-five yards. Pike also tied for the team lead in home runs—with zero. The fourth-place Brown Stockings finished first among six National Association teams that failed to homer all season.

And the rotation? What rotation? Rookie right-hander George Bradley started sixty of the team's seventy games and completed all but three. One could not imagine any pitcher in the modern era even approaching the 536 innings hurled by Bradley that season. Strangely, it was fellow rookie and St. Louis native Pud Galvin who at age eighteen served as his mound backup in 1875. He left after that year to embark on a Hall of Fame career while Bradley eventually faded into obscurity.

Bradley peaked during the inaugural season of the National League in 1876 with a 45–19 record and league-best 1.23 ERA while pitching all but four of the innings his team played. His prolific mound work was not uncommon for the period as throwing overhand was verboten. National League rules of the time dictated that "the ball must be delivered to the bat with the arm swinging nearly perpendicular at the side of the body, and the hand in swinging forward must pass below the hip." [1]

The Brown Stockings captured the championship of the fledgling NL that year despite finishing tied for second in the regular season. The *St. Louis Globe-Democrat* offered that the team in its town deserved the pennant after having beaten the first-place Chicago White Stockings in six of ten head-to-head clashes. The *Chicago Tribune* dismissed such a claim as ridiculous.

The result was an unofficial best-of-five series billed as "The Championship of the West" that featured scintillating pitching duels between Bradley and already legendary Chicago pitcher Albert Spalding. The hurlers traded shutouts in St. Louis before a spate of White Stocking errors before their home fans gave the Brown Stockings a 2–1 lead. *Tribune* writers, who had grown a bit antsy about their boasts of Chicago dominance, blamed the strong wind in the Windy City for the Game 3 defeat.

No such excuse could be excused as the tired pitchers squared off for the potential St. Louis clincher. The teams combined for a ridiculous thirty-nine runs in a 21–18 Brown Stockings victory that, at least in the hearts and minds and those of their fans, justified their assertion that they were indeed the king of the new National League. St. Louis newspapers gloated while denigrating the White Stockings as overpaid and living in Chicago as overpriced. "The only thing the 'Garden City' can beat us in is mortgages," joked the *Dispatch*.[2]

Chicago ownership figured if they could not beat Bradley, they could lure him away. And that they did before the 1877 season. But the joke was on them. He stumbled immediately into mediocrity and did not rebound to perform effectively until after leaving the White Stockings. But the loss of a lights-out Bradley and departure of Pike to Cincinnati sent the Brown Stockings reeling. They stumbled to a 28–32 finish in 1877.

That is when the history of the franchise becomes a bit murky. Some historians have claimed that the Brown Stockings offered contracts to four premier players from the Louisville Grays, all of whom had been implicated in a gambling scandal. The Grays held what appeared to be an insurmountable lead in the pennant race that year before suspiciously stumbling into a losing stretch that handed Boston the championship. The result was that several Grays players were summarily booted out of the National League. It has been asserted that some of them were offered contracts by the Brown Stockings, who had counted on them to sign, and that their inability to do so brought the realization that could not field a competitive team in 1878. The truth or fabrication of that story matters little—the bottom line is that the team folded. Their remaining players competed that year as amateurs. The organization suffered to the point of near extinction.

St. Louis remained out of professional baseball until local saloon-keeper Chris von der Ahe came to the rescue. The eccentric Prussian immigrant with a pronounced handlebar moustache understood the personal benefits of fans streaming to Grand Avenue Field near his bar on game days so he purchased the Brown Stockings and the ballpark in 1880. What better way to ensure business from patrons on hot summer afternoons? He renamed the team home Sportsman's Park and Club and placed it along with other venues owned by breweries and distilleries into the American Association, which was known for its rowdy, hard-drinking players.

Von der Ahe proved quite the promoter. He billed himself as "The Millionaire Sportsman" and "der Boss President" and lured fans in with on-site beer sales and sausages. He also bucked tradition and rankled many in the religious community by scheduling Sunday games. It was no

VON DER AHE - PRESIDENT ST. LOUIS

Local saloonkeeper Chris von der Ahe helped save baseball in St. Louis well before the turn of the twenty-first century. PHOTO COURTESY OF THE LIBRARY OF CONGRESS

wonder his teams, which he renamed the Browns in 1883, consistently led the league in attendance.[3]

Their success on the field certainly helped. St. Louis emerged as the most dominant team in the league throughout the decade. Von der Ahe boasted the foresight to utilize young baseball visionary Charles Comiskey as player-manager. Comiskey had proven his skills and talent for innovation as a pitcher and first baseman with Dubuque of the Northwest League in the late 1870s. Unlike others who played the latter position, he placed himself closer to second base to cut off balls heading into the hole. Some historians claim he was the first to work with pitchers on covering the bag on grounders he fielded.

Charles Comiskey had a huge impact on the franchise and on the sport.
PHOTO COURTESY OF THE LIBRARY OF CONGRESS

Von der Ahe signed him after an exhibition game in St. Louis in 1882 and paid him more than the contract stipulated. Comiskey never forgot that generosity. He returned the favor decades later by serving as a benefactor for von der Ahe after his former owner lost his fortune due to a series of bad investments. Comiskey had long before proven worth the extra money by taking over the managerial role full-time from old friend Ted Sullivan after a dispute with von der Ahe in 1883. The twenty-six-year-old took the job and ran with it, guiding St. Louis to four straight American Association championships and defeating legendary Cap Anson and his Chicago White Stockings in a six-game World Series in 1886.

Comiskey proved himself a far better manager than hitter early in his stint with the Browns. But he improved at the plate and became a terror on the basepaths. He peaked in 1887 by batting .335 with 103 RBI and 117 stolen bases. His performance paled in comparison to that of Canadian-born leftfielder James Edward "Tip" O'Neill, who captured the Triple Crown by batting a ridiculous .435 with fourteen home runs and 123 RBI. So legendary did O'Neill become that his nickname was used by future Speaker of the House Thomas "Tip" O'Neill. The Browns of that era regularly led the league in pitching behind Bob Caruthers, Dave Foutz, and Silver King, who used what was then a rare sidearm delivery to rack up forty-five victories in 1888 and twice win the ERA crown.

The death of the American Association a week before Christmas in 1891 proved devastating to the Browns. The league had lost clubs in its largest cities to the National League and talent to the NL and even the upstart Players League (including Comiskey), which promised higher salaries and had for one season wreaked havoc on the St. Louis team. Defections became so pronounced that the American Association merged with the National League.

St. Louis degenerated from best to worst overnight. Its heyday began fading from memory as a National League newbie. An era of ineptitude that would last two decades into the twenty-first century was about to begin.

Chapter Two

From Dominant to Doormat

The folding of the Players League after one historic season brought Comiskey back to St. Louis for one last hurrah in the dying American Association. But his departure had rankled von der Ahe and wrecked their relationship. Comiskey left to manage Cincinnati after the 1891 season, leaving the Browns with no proven leadership.

The result was a competitive catastrophe. They used five different managers in 1892 to lead a ragtag roster that had descended from one of the best at the plate and on the mound to among the worst. St. Louis finished ahead of only pathetic Baltimore in its first season in the National League.

One could hardly have imagined that the Browns could fall any further given their rich history. But they eventually regressed to become not only the lousiest team in baseball, but among the worst to ever don uniforms.

They certainly did not do justice to their new home. Seeking greener pastures for his team, von der Ahe accepted an offer from the Lindell Street Railway company to sign a fifteen-year lease to play at New Sportsman's Park. The venue, which cost a mere $45,000 to build and took up two city blocks, opened on April 27, 1893, with great fanfare. A parade from the Lindell Hotel featured the Italian American Cavalry and a coach pulled by four magnificent black horses from the stable of Gus Busch (whose son Gussie eventually owned the ballclub) reached its destination for Opening Day. Newcomers quickly noticed quite lopsided and distinct outfield dimensions—a cozy 290 feet from home plate to the fence in right field but 470 to left and 500 to center. Even the live-ball era would have precluded any possibility of anything but inside-the-park home runs slugged to those areas.

The Browns debuted in the National League that day with a 4–2 defeat of Louisville before a sellout crowd of 12,230. But any hopes of success approaching that of previous seasons were quickly dashed. An eleven-game losing streak set the club down a path of futility on which they remained for six years. Most pronounced was their feeble hitting. Player-manager Theodore Breitenstein even snared an ERA crown in 1893 despite a 19–24 record. St. Louis finished last or second-last in runs scored every year from 1893 to 1898.

The last of those campaigns was marred by a tragic event that all but nailed the coffin shut on von der Ahe's ownership. In the second inning of a game against Chicago a fan sitting in the wooden grand-stand dropped a lit cigar into a pile of canvas bags. The resulting fire was deemed as a mere nuisance at first, causing fans to move elsewhere in the ballpark and the umpires to stop the game to investigate. Other spectators grew impatient with the halt in action and began screaming for a resumption of play. Many believed the disturbance was the result of a fight in the stands.

They were sadly mistaken. The fire gained in intensity. Hundreds of fans scurried for one exit between the park and saloons but found to their horror that the gate was closed. Some forced their way through. Others were helped onto the playing field by players of both teams. About one hundred patrons were reported as injured. And, tragically, von der Ahe's greyhound dog, Fly, perished in the blaze. Workers busily rebuilt the fences and erected temporary stands overnight, allowing a game to be played the following day. The Browns likely wished it had been cancelled—they fell to the Chicago Orphans, 14–1. Such scores were typical for a St. Louis team that finished that season with a woeful 39–111–4 record.

With debts mounting, von der Ahe sold it to Cleveland Spiders owner Frank Robison in 1899. Robison had become disenchanted with fan support in that town. So, despite maintaining ownership of the Spiders, he simply moved his best players off that roster onto the St. Louis team he renamed the Perfectos, including immortal right-hander Cy Young. The plan aimed at vaulting the club into contention backfired on Robison. While the Spiders collapsed to sport what remains the worst record in major league baseball history at 20–134 the Perfectos proved far from dominant. They managed to place fifth at 84–67 after sprinting to the top of the standings behind Young, who won ten of his first eleven decisions. But Robison did rake in the bucks—attendance doubled at what became known as Robison Field as St. Louis ranked second in NL attendance.

The Perfectos might have ranked first in unruliness. Fights on the field and in the stands became so commonplace that police intervention was sometimes required. Robison claimed following one St. Louis defeat that disorder or even homicide could have resulted after the umpires refused to call the game due to rain. That came as no surprise. Robison and his players baited umpires unmercifully.

It certainly did not help. The Perfectos plummeted from first place in late May to fifth a month later and remained out of the race the rest of the way. Robison attempted to bolster the roster in 1900 by signing third baseman and future legendary Giants manager John McGraw and catcher Wilbert Robinson away from Baltimore. But though the former performed exceptionally, leading the league with a 505 on-base percentage, the team struggled as Robison and manager Patsy Tebeau squabbled incessantly. The owner begged McGraw to take over the reins but to no avail. McGraw returned to Baltimore in 1901 to play for the Orioles of the fledgling American League.

By that time the club had adopted its new nickname. Teams in that era became typically monikered based on uniform color. It has been asserted that *St. Louis Republic* writer Willie McHale was the first to refer to the team as the Cardinals in 1899. And though the beloved bird-on-the-bat logo was not created for another two decades, the Cardinals nickname had become official in 1900.

The advent of the American League in 1901 resulted in bidding wars over premier talent. McGraw and Robinson were not alone among key departures. The best to bolt was Young, who left for the new Boston franchise and lured talented battery mate Lou Criger with him. So desperate

Patsy Tebeau managed the club when the Perfectos became the Cardinals in 1900.
PHOTO COURTESY OF THE LIBRARY OF CONGRESS

was Robison to maintain legitimacy that he re-signed future Hall of Fame outfielder Jesse Burkett, who had won two batting totals with Cleveland and was nicknamed "The Crab" for his antisocial behavior. Burkett, who had all but decided to head elsewhere, proved himself still worth the money. He captured his third batting crown in 1901 at .376 and led the league in on-base percentage for the first time at .440.

Burkett led an attack that paced the National League in runs scored. The problem for the Cardinals was on the mound, where mediocrity reigned. The result was a late-summer collapse that dropped them from two to eleven games out of first place. The loss of Young had proven devastating.

That run of contention into August was recalled with relish soon after the 1902 season began. The Cardinals opened with three consecutive defeats to Pittsburgh, which left them in the dust. The Pirates bolted to a ridiculous 30–5 start while St. Louis dropped sixteen of its first twenty-two and remained, along with the rest of the National League, out of the race the rest of the way. The loss of Burkett and Hall of Fame third baseman Bobby Wallace to the Browns, the new crosstown team of the American League, had destroyed the offense. Robinson had filed a lawsuit to prevent their departures, but to no avail. The Cardinals, who led the league in attendance a year earlier, attracted 150,000 fewer fans to plummet to fourth in 1902.

The team was a mess. The loss of Burkett and Wallace continued to haunt the offense. St. Louis finished last in runs scored in 1903 while hitting just eight home runs, a meager total even in the dead-ball era. That was hardly enough to support a pitching staff that featured rookie right-hander Mordecai "Three-Finger" Brown, who led the team in ERA at 2.60 before taking his Hall of Fame talents to the Chicago Cubs in an ill-fated trade. The Cardinals suffered through one of the worst stretches of ineptitude in baseball history that year, dropping twenty-five of twenty-nine games in late April and May to cement their standing as the worst team in baseball.

Robison faced a dilemma. He believed Patsy Donovan had worn out his welcome as manager. But Donovan was the last productive hitter remaining. The owner allowed the Irish-born outfielder to latch on with the miserable Washington Senators of the American League, for whom he quickly ascended to player-manager.

His replacement at the helm in St. Louis was veteran pitcher Charles "Kid" Nichols, whose Hall of Fame career featured seven thirty-win seasons. The thirty-five-year-old right-hander not only achieved one last hurrah by serving as co-ace along with twenty-game winner Jack Taylor but he guided the Cardinals to a surprising turnaround. They fell out of contention in May but remained over .500 until dropping six straight to end the year. Nichols had returned optimism to the franchise and its fans as attendance nearly doubled.

The immortal Cy Young played just two seasons in St. Louis but managed to rack up forty-six victories.
PHOTO COURTESY OF THE LIBRARY OF
CONGRESS

But trouble was brewing behind the scenes. Nichols respected Robison but not the owner's son Stanley, who due to the failing health of his father had assumed greater control of the club. The younger Robison wasted little time firing Nichols after a slow start in 1905. The dismissal negatively affected the veteran on the mound. He had won just one decision with an ERA that had ballooned to 5.40 when he was released. The result was disastrous. The Redbirds collapsed so completely that managerial replacement Jimmy Burke was also canned in August and replaced by none other than Stanley Robison.

Robison did not exactly reach for the skies in picking his replacement. He plucked John McCloskey to take over his failing franchise. The obscure Kentuckian had not served as a major league manager for a decade, and even then only for one horrible year and another during which he was fired after compiling a 2–17 record.

One could have predicted the outcome. The club responded with one of the worst three-season stretches in baseball history. They hung around .500 through the quarter pole in 1906 then hit their stride as the lousiest team in the National League. They failed to win two consecutive games for the next five weeks, then lost eighteen of twenty-two to conclude the miserable campaign. Their lack of power was pronounced even with the sport stuck in the dead-ball era. The Cardinals hit just nine home runs and placed seventh in the eight-team league in doubles. Meanwhile, their pitching staff was devoid of an ace who could halt long losing streaks.

Those problems remained over the following two seasons as fans stayed away in droves. St. Louis averaged fewer than two hundred thousand fans to finish last in attendance in both. The club scored less than three runs per game during that stretch and bottomed out at a ridiculously meager 2.4 in 1908. Their feeble bats that year frustrated starting pitchers such as flash-in-the-pan Bugs Raymond and southpaw Johnny Lush, both of whom performed well despite losing records that reflected terrible run support.

That was the last straw for Robison, who fired McCloskey after that season. He sent Raymond and top hitter Red Murray to the New York Giants in a package that returned Hall of Fame catcher Roger Bresnahan with the intention of naming him player-manager. The move did not reap the fruits of success for which Robison hoped. Soon both he and Bresnahan had departed but in different ways. The long stretch of struggles continued.

CHAPTER THREE

Still a Mess

LEGENDARY GIANTS MANAGER JOHN MCGRAW WAS IN A GENEROUS state of mind in regard to Bresnahan. His catcher had served him well, and McGraw refused to block the desire of Bresnahan to become a major league manager. That is, as long as it did not hurt the Giants competitively.

The offer from St. Louis of Raymond, Murray, and promising catcher Admiral Schlei for the twenty-nine-year-old Bresnahan satisfied McGraw. It also satisfied Cardinals owner Stanley Robison—but not for long. The trade he expected to reverse the fortunes of his club served only to slightly improve its record. The team improved from historically bad to merely rotten.

Perhaps that should have come as little surprise given that Bresnahan was unproven as a skipper. He had certainly proven himself behind the plate and beyond. He had played all nine positions as a major leaguer and had established innovations in protective equipment as catcher. His speed, batting talent, and patience at the plate that resulted in walks and high on-base percentage forced McGraw to place him high in the Giants lineup rather than the eight spot traditionally occupied by catchers. It could be claimed that McGraw also liked Bresnahan for similar emotional traits. Both have been described as quick-tempered.

Bresnahan surrendered most of the catching duties to journeyman Ed Phelps to concentrate on managing. His absence weakened the lineup and prevented Bresnahan from finding a groove at the plate when he did play. He batted a career-worst .244 in 1909, though blossoming first baseman Ed Konetchy helped the Cardinals improve offensively. But the loss of Raymond and failures of Lush doomed the pitching staff to the worst ERA in the National League. The club performed respectably into early August before an epic collapse. St. Louis lost forty-one of fifty-eight games (including thirty-three of thirty-seven during one stretch) to end the season. Its fifteen-game losing streak in September remained its third-longest in franchise history through 2021.

Failing health prevented Robison from remaining fully active in seeking to better the roster. Only a trade for veteran second baseman and future Yankees Hall of Fame manager Miller Huggins constituted any off-season attempt to improve the club. Robison reaped what he sewed. The Cardinals performed a bit better in 1910 but managed only to escape the cellar. Any optimism launched by an eight-game winning streak in May was more than offset by a thirteen-game winless stretch in July and August.

Robison died in March 1911 after bequeathing control of the Cardinals to niece Helene Britton. That a woman was taking over a franchise alarmed many in the game. She was indeed the first female owner in major league baseball history. But they had plenty of time to brace for it—all her uncle's legal heirs were women. Britton tactfully offered a rebuttal to critics during an interview with *Baseball Magazine*.

"I realize that my positions as the only woman owner in the major leagues is a peculiar one," she said. "And I don't pretend to know the game as intimately from a playing standpoint as a man might do in my place. I appreciate the fact that baseball is a man's game, but I also appreciate the fact that women are taking an increasing interest in the sport which I believe is a healthy and wholly commendable sign."[1]

Britton expressed an interest in maintaining the status quo, at least at the top. Despite the inability of Bresnahan to transform them into anything close to a contender, she praised his work after taking over the organization. "I like his system," she said. "Indeed, I adore it, even if it has been climbing toward the first division . . . my great aim will be not to interfere with him."[2]

Her hands-off approach appeared to work in 1911. The Cardinals contended much of the year as attendance soared. Players in the everyday lineup followed Bresnahan's penchant for patience at the plate as

Helene Britton became the first female owner in major league history.
PHOTO COURTESY OF THE LIBRARY OF CONGRESS

the team led the league in on-base percentage. St. Louis won most of its close games in hanging around the periphery of the pennant race, even closing to within two games of first place in mid-July. Only a slump in late August and early September sealed their fate, but their fifth-place finish proved encouraging. So pleased was Britton with Bresnahan that she rewarded him with a five-year contract worth $10,000 annually, as well as 10 percent of the club's profits.

The positive feelings did not last long between the volatile manager and the fiercely independent owner. Their relationship became contentious as the losses piled up in 1912, the Cardinals lost ninety games, and attendance dropped by more than half. Frustration grew as the club lost most of the close games it had won in 1911. Among the disagreements centered on Bresnahan's desire to buy the team from Britton and her continued rejections. The final straw occurred when she criticized him after a defeat to the Cubs and, according to one report, he yanked his derby hat over his years and stomped off while proclaiming, "No woman can tell me how to play a ball game!" And when rumors persisted that Bresnahan had used an inferior lineup late that year against the Giants to help his friend McGraw win another pennant, the die was cast. Britton canned him and sent him packing to Chicago, where he played out his last three seasons and even served as Cubs manager in 1915.[3]

The firing divided the Cardinals into two camps. Some supported replacement Miller Huggins, who would eventually gain legendary status as a perennial champion manager of the New York Yankees. Others vented anger over the loss of Bresnahan. The result was a miserable season in which the Cardinals not only finished in the cellar but placed last in runs scored and allowed, as well as attendance. Fewer than three thousand fans per game graced Robison Field that year. Only the efforts of Huggins, who paced the National League in on-base percentage, and consistent ace pitcher Slim Sallee, prevented an even more disastrous campaign.

Huggins was a quiet person and deep thinker who preferred reading to socializing. He took seriously his managerial career and other business pursuits, such as his ownership of a cigar store and roller-skating rink. He studied the game and emerged quickly into an effective strategist, which impressed even the veterans of the sport such as McGraw. But the strain of losing in his first season nearly motivated him to quit. That small gate receipts gave his team little money to spend did not help. Over the next two years, Huggins was forced to supplement payroll out of his own pocket. The Cardinals appeared to be foundering heading into his second year at the helm. Another roadblock was the launching of the short-lived Federal League, which added competition for the sports dollar in St. Louis. The city now had three baseball teams, including the new Terriers and American League Browns. The Cardinals were fortunate that both were terrible.

Huggins—St. Louis National

Miller Huggins stopped off in St. Louis before emerging as a legendary manager with the New York Yankees.
PHOTO COURTESY OF THE LIBRARY OF CONGRESS

They were also fortunate that Huggins grew into the job and united his players. Britton did her job in 1914 by trading top hitter Ed Konetchy, who took his pro-Bresnahan bias to Pittsburgh in return for serviceable outfielders Cozy Dolan and Owen Wilson, as well as infielder Dots Miller, whose .290 batting average and eighty-eight RBI earned him NL Most Valuable Player votes.

The blossoming of young right-hander William "Poll" Perritt provided support for Sallee and budding right-hander Bill Doak in the rotation and helped transform the Cardinals into late-season contenders. Perritt and Sallee, who roomed together on the road and were inseparable, both won twice during a stretch in which the team took eight of nine to vault to within one game of first place. They remained a pennant threat into mid-September before faltering.

What Britton and Huggins built up quickly came crashing down. The centerpiece of the collapse proved to be Perritt, who declined a three-year contract offer for $12,000—a comparatively hefty sum at the time. Rumors swirled that Perritt was being courted by Pittsburgh manager Rebel Oakes of the Federal League—the two were friends who had grown up just twenty miles apart in Louisiana. Angered by the rejection, St. Louis management began spreading rumors that Perritt was a drinker whose laziness on the field limited production. The claim of weak effort was absurd—he had finished the season with a sparkling 2.36 ERA.

Perritt left the Cardinals the same day he received bonus money for their third-place finish. Schuyler Britton—the owner's husband and team president—wasted no time cancelling the check, leading to a bitter argument. Perritt soon accepted Britton's dare to sue. That put Huggins in the eye of the storm. He refused to lose Perritt for nothing, so the team traded him to McGraw and the Giants for next to nothing. The infamous "player to be named later" received by St. Louis proved to be fading outfielder Bob Bescher, who managed two mediocre seasons with his new club.

The Giants signed Perritt to a three-year deal, which angered Oakes, who met Perritt in a St. Louis café and became combative for breaking a contract with Pittsburgh. That individual case of team-jumping helped motivate Major League Baseball to strengthen the reserve clause that tied players to their teams in perpetuity. That lack of freedom remained rock solid until the advent of free agency in the 1970s.

The experience deeply affected the Brittons' business practices. They refused to lure back any player deemed disloyal for bolting the team for the Federal League after that renegade organization folded in 1915. While their rivals bolstered their rosters with fine talent the Cardinals fell apart. By 1916, they suffered from the weakest hitting and pitching in the National League. And it cost them dearly—figuratively and literally. An average of fewer than three thousand fans trickled into Robison Field that year.

But one bright light emerged during that dark season. And that was Rogers Hornsby, who split time between shortstop and third base but would eventually make his mark in the outfield. He had been spotted two years earlier by Cardinals scout Bob Connery, who was immediately impressed with the way the kid fielded tough hops at Class D Denison. And though Connery was proven wrong about defensive efficiency— Hornsby committed a whopping fifty-eight errors that season in the minors—the scout had certainly discovered an amazing hitter.

The nineteen-year-old arrived for a cup of coffee in 1915 before easily leading the feeble Cardinals in batting average, RBI, and triples the following year. His .313 mark was, incredibly and sadly, sixty-seven points higher than that of any teammate. Hornsby and a baseball legend were about to take the franchise out of its misery. And so was an owner who had earned big bucks decades earlier selling those newfangled contraptions called automobiles.

CHAPTER FOUR

Rogers and Rickey

IT WAS 1902. SCHOOL DROPOUT SAMUEL BREADON HAD TAKEN A JOB TO help his immigrant mother make ends meet after his father died. The family lived in a tough neighborhood near the docks in Greenwich Village. One of eight children, young Samuel eventually landed a gig as a bank clerk on Wall Street earning $125 a month.

Breadon followed the advice of another New Yorker. It was newspaper editor Horace Greeley, after all, who in 1865 famously said, "Go west, young man." And Breadon did. He and his brothers moved to St. Louis in 1902 to open a car dealership and garage. He understood the risk of the new industry but foresaw it as the wave of the future. But brotherly love became strained when his siblings fired Samuel upon hearing that he planned to break away and open his own shop.

That fear had been premature. Samuel did not have enough money to launch a business. So, he gained a popcorn concession at the 1904 St. Louis World's Fair to earn it. Breadon opened his own garage. Then Dame Fortune smiled at him. A wealthy customer who appreciated his industriousness and honesty offered him an executive position with the Western Automobile Company. Breadon ran with it. He eventually bought the company and co-owned a Pierce-Arrow distributorship.

By that time, the huge Cardinals fan had become a minority owner of the club. He owned 51 percent of the franchise by 1919. For the first time in decades, the St. Louis team was on solid financial footing. And it showed on the field. Dominance and the Gas House Gang glory would have to wait several years. But the Breadon era brought immediate respect.

Sam Breadon made mountains of money owning the franchise for three decades.
PHOTO COURTESY OF THE BASEBALL HALL OF FAME AND MUSEUM

Among the key figures in the rebound was manager Branch Rickey, who would earn far greater historical notoriety a quarter-century later with the Brooklyn Dodgers when he boldly integrated major league baseball by signing Jackie Robinson. The former St. Louis Browns manager, who had served as president of the Cardinals, took over the managerial position as well after firing Huggins, with whom he clashed over baseball strategy. The motivation for taking a second job within the cash-strapped organization was purely to save it another salary.

Rickey faced a tough task. St. Louis had not sported back-to-back winning records since 1891. The team required more than production from Rogers Hornsby to score enough runs to win consistently. It boasted no ace pitcher who could halt losing streaks.

Branch Rickey laid the groundwork for success as manager of the Cardinals in the early 1920s.
PHOTO COURTESY OF THE LIBRARY OF CONGRESS

The new skipper discovered the depth of his challenge the hard way in 1919. Though veteran infielder Milt Stock aided Hornsby offensively he hit no home runs. Neither did anybody else—the budding superstar slugged eight of the team's seventeen total homers. The Cardinals finished seventh of eight teams in both runs scored and team ERA that season to finish with a dismal 54–83–1 record.

Rickey went to work. He astutely signed first baseman Jack Fournier, who had been waived by the White Sox after several strong seasons after that team picked up Chick Gandil, who would later be implicated in the Black Sox scandal and banned from baseball. Fournier was an immediate hit as a hitter in St. Louis, batting .305 and placing second on the team with seventy-seven runs scored in 1920. Rickey also acquired starting pitcher Jesse Haines from Cincinnati. The right-hander launched his

Hall of Fame career that season, teaming up with Bill Doak to form a strong one-two punch on the mound.

The Cardinals were about to fly as the dead ball era was about to die. And they began to bash home runs in their new home. They started sharing Sportsman's Park with the American League Browns on July 1, 1920. The friendlier dimensions between the fence and home plate, which were between fifty and one hundred feet closer than at the crumbling firetrap known as Robison Field, proved ideal for such sluggers as Hornsby, Fournier, and young outfielder Austin McHenry, whose promising career was cut short when a brain tumor took his life at age twenty-seven. St. Louis placed second in the National League in home runs in 1921 with eighty-three. Meanwhile, Haines and Doak headed a vastly improved pitching staff.

It took time for the Redbirds to jell. But they played as well as any team in baseball down the stretch. Fueled by brilliant pitching they won twenty of twenty-three games in late August and early September to vault into the outskirts of the pennant race and finished the season on a 32–10 tear.

Optimism seemed warranted when the Cardinals arrived in training camp in 1922. And fans were in for a bit of a surprise when they caught a glimpse of their baseball heroes, courtesy of Rickey. The club vice president, general manager, and manager had been inspired during a speaking engagement in mid-February at the Men's Fellowship Club of the Ferguson (Missouri) Presbyterian Church. Among the decorations he noted was a cardboard cutout of red cardinal birds perched atop twigs made of string. The image proved visionary for Rickey, who took it to the head of the art department at the Woodword and Tiernan Printing Company, which transformed it into the legendary "birds on the bat" logo that remained on Cardinals uniforms a century. The lone exceptions were 1926, when a single bird was used, and in 1956, when the birds on the bat disappeared.

The new design was praised by the media, as was the team after a 10–1 thrashing of Pittsburgh in the 1922 season opener, which attracted eighteen thousand fans to Sportsman's Park. Offered poetic *St. Louis Post-Dispatch* columnist L.C. Davis:

*The Cardinals' new uniform Will take the populace by storm—For they
are sure a classy bunch of dressers. They'll set the pace, likewise the style.
And win the pennant by a mile Unless the local fans are rotten guessers.*[1]

To equate a popular new logo with certainty of a runaway champion
was absurd, but the team appeared destined most of the season to remain
the race wire-to-wire. The Cardinals could not claim to be the New York
Yankees of the National League in ushering in the live ball era, but they
did mash 107 home runs to rank second in the senior circuit as Hornsby
clobbered forty-two to set a franchise record. They led one and all with
280 doubles and finished behind only Pittsburgh in runs scored. Every
starter in the lineup batted at least .292, though in that burgeoning era
of offensive explosion their .301 team mark placed them only third in
the National League. St. Louis might have won the crown if not for the
collapse of Doak, whose ERA more than doubled from the previous year
when he sported the lowest in the league.

The 1922 Cardinals took advantage of early balance in the National
League to remain alive despite barely staying over .500 into June. Then
they sizzled. They won seventeen of twenty during what would today be
considered a ridiculously long twenty-three-game homestand to vault
into the lead. They remained in first place into mid-August before losing
thirteen of eighteen on another long stretch at Sportsman's Park to fall
out of the race. Doak played the role of goat during the collapse, losing
all four of his decisions and allowing nineteen runs in nineteen innings.

Doak was traded to the Dodgers two years later but had made his
mark in baseball history. He was not only nicknamed "Spittin' Bill" as one
of the last legal spitball pitchers in the major leagues, but he also invented
the webbed glove that served as more of a net than the pancake models
of the past, which were intended only to protect the hand and were not
conducive to easily handling baseballs fired in their direction, especially
those of the harder variety during the live ball era.

Rickey believed his team boasted enough offense to trade Fournier
and replace him at first base with promising rookie Jim Bottomley. The
manager and GM was both right and wrong. Bottomley indeed proved
in 1923 he was ready for the big time. The future Hall of Famer exploded

onto the scene by batting .371 and driving in ninety-four runs. But the Cardinals lost the deal that sent Fournier to Brooklyn for outfielder Hi Myers and first baseman Ray Schmandt. Fournier blossomed into a productive power hitter in the Big Apple while Myers hit only for average in St. Louis and Schmandt retired rather than report to his new team.

The result was lost power and a precipitous drop offensively. The Redbirds returned to mediocrity as disenchanted fans stayed away. But that proved to be a glorious season compared to 1924 despite tremendous performances from Hornsby, Bottomley, and flash-in-the-pan outfielder Ray Blades. The club's inability to develop or land a premier pitcher doomed that edition. St. Louis used fifteen different starters that year in a vain attempt to find a consistent winner.

Breadon canned Rickey as manager after a terrible 13–25 start in 1925 as some questioned his leadership skills but the owner showed the common sense to maintain his position as general manager. Rickey felt humiliated over the firing but resisted the temptation to leave the club. He had become frustrated over losing talent to NL competitors. So, he took a bold step that resulted in the creation of the farm system. He took over the minor league Houston club and deemed it to be in the Cardinals organization. Rickey was not attempting to be revolutionary, as he explained nearly a decade later to *Sporting News* writer Dick Farrington.

"When the Cardinals were fighting for their life in the National League, I found that we were at a disadvantage in obtaining players of merit from the minors," he said. "Other clubs could outbid. They had money. They had superior scouting machinery. In short, we had to take what was left or nothing at all. . . . Thus it was that we took over the Houston club for a Class A proving ground. Still, I do not feel that the farming system we have established is the result of any inventive genius—it is the result of stark necessity. We did it to meet a question of supply and demand of young ballplayers."[2]

The plan worked. The Cardinals eventually emerged as the strongest franchise in the National League, a distinction that one could argue they have maintained ever since. They were about to embark on their first world championship run. But it was not a kid groomed in Houston who would lead the way. It was their new player-manager, who had developed into arguably the greatest right-handed hitter of all time.

CHAPTER FIVE

The History of Hornsby

WHEN ROGERS HORNSBY STEPPED INTO THE BATTER'S BOX FOR HIS first major league at-bat against a Cincinnati right-hander with the Shakespearean name of King Lear on September 15, 1915, it seemed impossible that he could ever hit a home run. Hornsby was 135 pounds, he crouched over the plate, and he choked up on the bat. After all, fences were distant in that era, and he displayed virtually no power. Logic told one that Hornsby would only circle the bases on an inside-the-park variety.

Little could anyone have imagined that he would blossom into perhaps not only the best pure hitter in National League history, but a prolific home run champion in the live ball era. Hornsby would never rival Babe Ruth or several other contemporaries as a slugger, but he would take a back seat to no one in overall production.

Such greatness might never have achieved had Hornsby not taken literally a threat uttered to him by manager Miller Huggins after receiving a cup of coffee that fateful September with the Cardinals and batted just .246. "I think, son, that you should be farmed out," Huggins told him.

Hornsby misunderstood. He figured Huggins wanted him to spend the offseason working on a farm to gain size and strength, so he did just that. He toiled on his uncle's farm and added thirty pounds of muscle. Huggins had unwittingly but happily created a monster. Hornsby finished his career with a .358 batting average that has remained, a century later, the second-best in major league history, eight points behind that of the immortal Ty Cobb.

Rogers Hornsby was arguably the greatest pure hitter in National League history, but he also developed power as his career moved along.

PHOTO COURTESY OF THE BASEBALL HALL OF FAME AND MUSEUM

Hornsby was an ancestor of many who traveled dangerous routes from Georgia to Texas during the rugged days of nineteenth-century Western expansion, some of whom were even killed by bands of Comanches. Among their offspring who settled in Travis County, which rests twelve miles from the state capital of Austin, was Ed Hornsby. He married Mary Dallas Rogers from nearby Rogers Hill in 1882. The couple eventually settled in Runnels County to raise cattle and have children, including redheaded, blue-eyed Rogers, who was born on April 27, 1896.

The young Hornsby would never know his father, who died when he was just two years old. Mary soon took herself and five kids to live with her mother on a farm back in Travis County. It was in a field by a nearby river that Rogers first learned how to play baseball. He embraced the challenge of competing against older kids and became obsessed with the sport.

That passion only intensified when the family traded a rural life for a city one in growing North Fort Worth after the turn of the century. He recalled years later playing only baseball with his elementary-school friends. He even spoke about leading a local team complete with blue flannel uniforms at age nine and traveling in trolley cars to games against clubs from other neighborhoods.

The burgeoning sport embraced in the early 1900s by kids throughout America drove Hornsby. A baseball career was considered by many adults neither lucrative nor a classy ambition, but it inspired millions. Hornsby showed potential with his coordination and fielding ability, even serving as a substitute player on teams consisting of adult stockyards and packing-plant workers at age ten. His confidence eventually grew to the point of cockiness.

A huge boom in the population of Fort Worth coincided with the exponential growth of amateur baseball teams in the area as the second decade of the twenty-first century approached. Hornsby competed in both baseball and football at North Side High School. His star teammate on the gridiron was Bo McMillin, who later played in the NFL and coached the Philadelphia Eagles and Detroit Lions. But family obligations forced Hornsby to drop out of school after just two years and take a job as an office boy at a local meat-packing plant.

His motivation was not merely financial. Hornsby had set his sights on a baseball career and played for the stockyard team, as well as other clubs around Fort Worth. But he was not wowing anyone. Though his fielding talent was pronounced, he was so painfully thin that he admitted to struggle swinging the bat. Unlike other mothers around the country who pushed their sons away from athletic careers, his mom encouraged him to play as often as possible and pursue his dream.

Older son Everett had already reached the professional level as a pitcher, though he never earned a spot in the big leagues. He arranged a tryout for his kid brother with the low-minor Dallas Steers, who signed Rogers to a contract in 1914. That opportunity proved fruitless—he sat on the bench for two weeks before his release. He landed with Class D Hugo of the rock-bottom Texas-Oklahoma League only to lose that job when the franchise folded, then hooked up with the Denison Railroaders. He finally received significant playing time there but committed forty-five errors in 113 games and batted just .232. Those were not numbers to place on a résumé. He begged Denison teammate and future major-leaguer Herb Hunter, "Will somebody teach me how to hit?"[1] His career appeared to be going nowhere.

Appearances can be deceiving. Hornsby was fortunate the cash-strapped Cardinals were around. Huggins told lone team scout Bob Connery that since the club could not afford to pay high-level minor league talent, he should find players with potential from lower-level leagues. He stumbled upon Hornsby during a series of exhibitions in small towns. Hornsby did not hit much, but Connery struck with him as a second baseman. "The more I looked at the kid, the better I liked him," the scout recalled years later. "He was green and awkward but possessed a great pair of hands. He fielded bad hoppers neatly and got the ball away quickly."[2]

Hornsby didn't do much else upon his eventual arrival with the Cardinals as another lousy season concluded in 1915. He also felt over-whelmed living in a huge city in comparison to North Fort Worth at that time. He often found himself lost as he navigated the neighborhoods around the boardinghouse in which he lived.

And though Hornsby, who had by that time moved to shortstop, felt far more at home on the baseball diamond, he remained impotent with bat in hand. Despite his 135-pound frame, he still clutched the bat at the end and took big swings. Huggins and Connery eventually convinced him to choke up and crowd the plate for superior coverage while gaining a better ability to hit to the opposite field. Yearning to see more, the manager started Hornsby in each of the last fifteen games down the stretch. The kid did not exactly set the field on fire. He managed only two extra-base hits and committed eight errors, annoying and angering his teammates in the process.

Hornsby had certainly not earned a starting job heading into the 1916 season. His outlook seemed even bleaker when the Cardinals signed young shortstop and eventual bust Roy Corhan from the Pacific Coast League and proclaimed him the starter. The influx of available talent from the doomed Federal League also weakened Hornsby's prospects.

But Huggins was in for a shock when his team opened camp in the sleepy Texas village of Hot Wells. Not only had Hornsby gained thirty pounds, but he had returned to his old batting style. That might have angered Huggins had the teenager not consistently slammed line drives all over the field to land the everyday shortstop position. The contrast in age and achievement was spotlighted in the April 12 season opener, when the Pirates and legendary shortstop Honus Wagner arrived at Robison Field. But it was Hornsby who stole the show. He drove in both St. Louis runs in a victory.

Hornsby was soon shifted to third base—he did not settle in as a full-time second baseman until 1920. But he always made a far more positive impact at the plate. He raised his batting average to .300 before midseason in 1916 to move from seventh to cleanup in the batting order, a shockingly rapid rise given his previous offensive struggles. He remained in the race for a National League batting title until a late-September slump.

Rivals of the financially strapped Redbirds circled like vultures. They wanted Hornsby. But management understood that the young star would draw fans and help transform the team into a winner. And he eventually did. But not before ruffling a few Cardinal feathers, particularly when Huggins bolted to manage the Yankees and was replaced in 1918 by Jack Hendricks, whom he called a "boob." Hornsby allowed his growing ego to destroy his relationship with teammates, even claiming after refusing to slide on a play at home plate in which he was tagged out that, "I'm too good a ballplayer to be sliding for a tail-end team."[3]

It can be claimed that his dissatisfaction affected his play. He batted what would prove to be an uncharacteristic .281 in 1918 while committing a whopping forty-six errors—mostly at shortstop—in 115 games. During the offseason, while toiling at a shipyard in Delaware that was aiding the war effort and awaiting his wedding with fiancée, Sarah, he stated emphatically that he would not play another year under Hendricks. Management understood on which side their bread was buttered so they canned Hendricks and installed Rickey as both manager and team president.

Teammates believed Hornsby cared nothing about his fielding though the task of improving proved more difficult when Rickey moved him from one infield position to another and Hornsby did lower his error totals as the seasons progressed. The Cardinals were certainly not ready to part with their superstar despite overtures from the Giants, who in one conversation offered $70,000 and four players and in another proposed a straight cash deal for $300,000. Both were tempting for a club still struggling competitively and financially. But they were rejected.

Rickey finally placed Hornsby at second base in 1920 and kept him there. He led all National League second basemen with thirty-four errors, but his continued defensive shortcomings were more than offset by his bat. Hornsby rose his average from an excellent .319 the previous year to an otherworldly .370 to not just win the batting title and lead the league in hits, doubles, and RBI, but this also set him on the path of offensive excellence arguably unmatched in the annals of baseball history.

Hornsby indeed adapted to the live ball era like a duck takes to water. Though his level of impact on the sport could not compete with that of Babe Ruth in the American League, who remained unmatched as a home run slugger, it can be argued that Hornsby was equally dominant. He thrice exceeded .400 over the next six seasons, a stretch in which he hit an incredible .397 overall. Hornsby remained through 2021 the only National League hitter to bat .400 in three different years. His .424 mark in 1924 remains the highest in the modern era. And despite never approaching Ruth as a power hitter, he did pace the senior circuit in slugging percentage in each of those seasons and twice in home runs. No less an authority than Ted Williams claimed that Hornsby was "the greatest hitter for average and power in the history of baseball."[4]

Those who complained that Hornsby did not take his fielding seriously certainly could not assert the same about his hitting or his career in general. Unlike most of his compatriots he did not drink, smoke, or party, though he gambled on the horses occasionally and his marriage collapsed when his wife discovered his affair with a married woman, whom he wed in 1924. Hornsby displayed an intensity as a ballplayer and passion for winning that made him alienated by his peers. His personality became particularly intolerable as a first-year manager in 1926, his last season with St. Louis. Wrote author Anthony J. Connor in the 1984 book *Voices from Cooperstown*:

> *He was a real hard-nosed guy. He ran the clubhouse like a Gestapo camp. You couldn't smoke, drink a soft drink, eat a sandwich. Couldn't read a paper. When you walked in the clubhouse you put your uniform on and got ready to play. What was it! No more kidding around, no joking, no laughing. He was dedicated to the game and made sure you were too. A very serious person.*[5]

That abrasiveness eventually caused Hornsby to wear out his welcome with the Cardinals. He even irritated the usually mild-mannered Rickey, whom he physically attacked twice in 1923 after accusing the superstar of faking an ailment that limited him to 107 games. Never mind that Hornsby was dealing with a knee injury and severe skin rash. The deteriorating relationship opened Rickey up to trade talks with McGraw and the still-interested Giants but the St. Louis insistence that hard-hitting infielder Frankie Frisch be included nixed the deal. Cardinals owner Sam Breadon also turned down a straight cash offer from the Brooklyn Robins.

Hornsby remained a loner. He avoided socializing with teammates and interviews with the media after games. He showered and bolted quickly. He also preferred rooming by himself on the road. But his production on the field overwhelmed any personal negatives. The organization understood his value. He signed after his absurd 1924 season a three-year contract for what was then an astronomical $100,000. Only Babe Ruth earned more among ballplayers.

Rickey and Hornsby eventually patched up their differences enough to move forward. The former was fired as manager thirty-eight games into the 1925 season but retained his position as general manager. Breadon convinced Hornsby to grab the reins on the field. He transformed the club into a winner. The focus on managing, including in-game strategies, did not affect Hornsby at the plate. He hit .403 to capture his sixth-consecutive National League batting title.

But a storm was brewing. Though his team embarked in 1926 on its first pennant and World Series championship, nagging injuries sent his average plummeting to .317. The death of his mother at the comparatively tender age of sixty-two, just before the Fall Classic dampened the thrill. And despite the praise he earned and received for his managerial skills from players and sportswriters his time with the Cardinals proved short. Hornsby asked the club to tear up the contract he signed just a year earlier and replace it with one that paid him a whopping $50,000 per season. Breadon countered with a one-year offer for that amount with a stipulation that Hornsby abstain from betting on the horses.

Indeed, that vice negatively impacted his life and career. The activity had alarmed the organization and major league baseball following the 1919 Black Sox Scandal, in which the White Sox threw the World Series and nearly ruined the sport. His gambling habit became public through his involvement with betting agent Frank Moore. He required Moore to make himself available to place bets for him. Hornsby even invited Moore to spring training in 1926, causing Breadon to publicly denounce his star player. But that did not deter Hornsby from hanging around Moore constantly as a gambling companion. The issue further strained an already-tenuous relationship.

The seeds of discontent had long since been planted. Among the disagreements between Hornsby and Breadon centered on an exhibition game scheduled for his exhausted club during the September run for the pennant. Hornsby voiced his displeasure angrily to the owner, then to the press. Breadon marched into Rickey's office and demanded that Hornsby be sent packing. "How can I trade this man now . . . and for whom?" the general manager replied.[6]

Little did the superstar know that the owner had a contingency plan. Breadon understood that McGraw and the Giants remained steadfast in their desire to land Hornsby. He was also aware that McGraw had not only become disenchanted with Frisch but had often verbally abused him after defeats in front of his teammates. Frisch had accepted the mistreatment in the belief that it was intended to inspire his fellow players. But after a particularly galling diatribe in late 1926, he left the club and returned home to New York.

The die was cast. Two stars who had worn out their welcomes seemed destined to be swapped for each other. And indeed, they were, two months after St. Louis snagged its first crown. Breadon sent Hornsby to New York for Frisch and cooked right-hander Jimmy Ring, whom Breadon claimed every National League team wanted but performed horribly in losing all four decisions for St. Louis in 1927 before being unloaded to Philadelphia.

Breadon stated later it was his intention all along, as he hoped his star would reject the one-year offer. "If they want to trade me, it's all right with me, but it doesn't look right that I should be traded from a club that I just managed to a world's championship," Hornsby said. "I gave the Cardinals all I had, and I asked for a contract that I believe I was entitled to."[7]

The deal infuriated St. Louis fans. One group hung crepe on Breadon's office door. Another jumped on the running board of his car to shout insults. But the performance of Frisch in years to come vindicated the owner. Hornsby never landed a contract for $50,000. He performed brilliantly for one season in the Big Apple before a trade to the Braves, then the Cubs. He returned for a cameo with the Cardinals in 1933 and concluded his career with the crosstown Browns. A heel injury and problems with teammates and management prevented him from playing full-time beyond 1929. Meanwhile, Frisch remained steady and productive as a key contributor to the great Gas House Gang. Breadon had dealt Hornsby for the right player at the right time.

Yet despite all the personal issues Rogers Hornsby would go down in history along with Stan Musial as the greatest Cardinals hitter of the twentieth century.

CHAPTER SIX

The First Cardinal Crown

THE APPROACH OF THE 1926 SEASON CAUSED FEW CARDINAL FANS TO rub their hands in gleeful anticipation. Granted, their favorite team had rebounded the previous season under new manager Rogers Hornsby to inch above .500. Hornsby and lineup mates Jim Bottomley and Ray Blades had long established themselves as productive offensively. But the old axiom that good pitching beats good hitting promised to prevent St. Louis from joining the pennant race. Top starters Jesse Haines and Bill Sherdel had performed like yo-yos—up one year and down the next. None of their fellow hurlers seemed destined to emerge as a badly needed ace.

Nothing the Cardinals did through May changed the minds of the doomsayers. They had even regressed from 1925, falling into sixth place with a 23–25 record. They were in the midst of what would today be an unheard-of twenty-two-game road trip. But they suddenly got hot. White-hot. They swept Philadelphia. They swept New York. They swept Boston. They won twelve of thirteen to catapult to within a half-game of first place. And though they slumped soon thereafter, they remained in the race the rest of the way. They had become road warriors. Another sizzling stretch away from home in early August featured a rare six-game sweep of Brooklyn and launched a 16–2 tear that placed them atop the National League.

A four-team fight to the finish had begun. Soon Chicago and Pittsburgh faded. Only Cincinnati remained an obstacle as the Redbirds sought their first pennant since joining the league in 1892. The Reds won eight straight in mid-September to forge a tie. But they did not win another game for a week. And when Sherdel pitched eight brilliant innings in relief against the Giants in the Polo Grounds on September 24, the Cardinals had secured the crown.

St. Louis went crazy. Jubilant fans honked car horns and tossed confetti from buildings. Some literally danced in the streets. Few had dared dream at season's start that their team could capture the National League championship.

The front office had done its part in June. General manager Branch Rickey shrewdly traded for thirty-nine-year-old right-hander Grover Cleveland Alexander, a future Hall of Famer whom the Cubs assumed based on diminishing returns was done. Alexander outperformed all other St. Louis starters, quite an achievement considering flash-in-the-pan Flint Rhem was on his way to leading the league with twenty wins, and both Haines and Sherdel were enjoying fine seasons. Rickey also acquired aging-but-still-productive outfielder Billy Southworth, another player headed for Cooperstown. He added punch to a lineup destined to lead the NL in runs scored.

The death of Hornsby's mother as the team prepared to play the vaunted Yankees in the World Series proved more an inspiration than impediment to a title. She requested after the Cardinals clinched the pennant that her funeral be held after the Fall Classic.

The question immediately asked: Could the St. Louis pitchers rein in Murderer's Row? The answer: Often enough. They limited New York to just four home runs in the seven-game series. All were slugged by Babe Ruth, including three in a 10–5 rout in Game 4 to famously fulfill his promise to young boy Johnny Sylvester, who had been hospitalized after being tossed to the ground and kicked in the head by a horse. The Cardinals held their typically explosive foe to thirteen runs in the other six games combined. That dominance was remarkable given that Rehm, who was relegated to fourth starter despite his 20–7 record in the regular season, was knocked out early in that lopsided defeat after surrendering two blasts by the Great Bambino.

A ten-inning defeat in Game 5 that featured a taut pitcher's duel between Sherdel and Yankees ace Herb Pennock placed St. Louis on the

Immortal pitcher Grover Cleveland Alexander was approaching forty by the time he reached St. Louis, but he won twenty-one games in 1927.
PHOTO COURTESY OF THE BASEBALL HALL OF FAME AND MUSEUM

brink of elimination. But Alexander came to the rescue before nearly fifty thousand fans at Yankee Stadium. He hurled a complete-game victory that hot-hitting first baseman Les Bell put away with a three-run homer. A showdown for the crown at what would become the most legendary venue in American sport was set for the following afternoon.

That Alexander would be called upon to play the role of hero again came as a surprise. Not only had he pitched wire-to-wire the previous day, but he was a notorious drinker. All who knew him assumed he had celebrated his victory by boozing it up and would arrive at the ballpark with a hangover. The possibility appeared even more remote when a defensive collapse by the Yankees in the fourth inning led to a 3–1 St. Louis lead and Haines continued to mow down the opposition. But when New York cut its deficit to one and loaded the bases against the right-hander in the seventh, Hornsby shocked the baseball world by summoning Alexander from the bullpen. Little did the outside world know that the manager had instructed the pitcher to stay sober the previous night in case he was needed the next day.

The thirty-nine-year-old nicknamed "Old Pete" didn't pitch like old anyone. He struck out dangerous rookie and future Hall of Famer Tony Lazzeri to kill the rally. Lazzeri nearly doomed the Cardinals with a grand slam, but his shot curved foul, proving once again that baseball is a game of inches. "Less than a foot made the difference between a hero and a bum," Alexander said.[1]

Soon arrived a ninth inning that would go down as one of the most exciting and perplexing endings in baseball history. Alexander opened the frame by retiring premier hitters Earle Combs and Mark Koenig. He walked Ruth—Hornsby had ordered after Game 4 that all his hurlers pitch around him. But with the immortal Lou Gehrig at the plate, Ruth tried to take Alexander by surprise and steal second (though some historians believe it was a failed hit-and-run). Catcher Bob O'Farrell fired a bullet to Hornsby, who tagged Ruth out easily. The Cardinals were world champions. "Ruth didn't say a word," Hornsby reported as his team celebrated. "He didn't even look around or up at me. He just picked himself up and walked away."[2]

Alexander didn't walk away figuratively. He could have gone out on top but instead felt reinvigorated. He continued to perform for St. Louis like the Alexander of old, sporting records of 21–10 and 16–9 the next two seasons beyond the age of forty. So legendary had he become that Hollywood made a film of his life posthumously in 1952 starring future president Ronald Reagan.

The Cardinals took advantage of his continued greatness after a successful trade of Hornsby for second baseman Frankie Frisch that resulted in O'Farrell being named player-manager. They won more games in 1927 than they had during their championship run. They chased the Pirates all year but could not catch them despite winning twenty-nine of forty-two games to finish the season. Frisch did not match Hornsby's power but performed brilliantly, leading the team in batting average (.337), runs scored (112), and stolen bases (48). St. Louis pitching picked up where it left off in 1926 as Haines managed a career-high in wins and career-low in ERA as a full-time starter.

O'Farrell had never felt comfortable at the helm. He often ceded decision-making during games to coach Bill McKechnie, who had been fired by Pittsburgh after five years despite leading that team to the 1925 world championship. McKechnie replaced O'Farrell as manager in 1928. That is when a reversal of fortunes began. This time it was the competition chasing in vain. The blossoming of Chick Hafey, yet another Hall of Famer who spent most of his career with the club, completed a powerful offensive triumvirate. Playing every day after graduating from his four-year status as a part-timer, Hafey paced the team in batting average at .337 with twenty-seven home runs and 111 RBI to supplement the typically potent Frisch and Bottomley, who earned Most Valuable Player honors by leading the league in triples, home runs, and RBI. The bespectacled Hafey, whose playing time had been limited by various ailments, thrived as a regular in 1928.

The Cardinals needed every win down the stretch with the Giants and Cubs in hot pursuit. Two defeats to the former in late September before ninety thousand fans in New York narrowed their lead to one game. But they won six of their next seven, including the pennant-clincher against the woeful Braves behind Sherdel. A World Series rematch against the vengeful and even more powerful Yankees was set.

Still embarrassed by the baserunning blunder that ended the 1926 battle, Ruth proved unstoppable. In one of the greatest hitting displays in baseball history, he slammed ten hits, including three home runs, in just sixteen at-bats, to lead a four-game sweep. Ruth and Gehrig combined to batter St. Louis pitching with a ridiculous .593 batting average, seven homers, and thirteen RBI. New York outscored its overwhelmed foe by at least three runs in all four games.

Breadon reacted after McKechnie lost the World Series as he did with Hornsby after that superstar won it. He got rid of him. Breadon did not just can McKechnie. He swapped McKechnie with Southworth, who had managed the Rochester club to the International League title. The latter was woefully inexperienced, having managed just one season in the minors.

And it showed in 1929. Breadon, who had hired his fourth manager in four years despite the unparalleled success of the franchise, had placed Southworth in the awkward position of taking charge of those who two years earlier had been his friends. The owner believed McKechnie had been too soft on his players. He instructed Southworth to inject greater toughness and discipline.

The plan backfired. The Cardinals rejected their new authority figure. Southworth ran them ragged in spring training. They toiled longer hours than any other club. They weren't even allowed to leave to grab lunch elsewhere and take it back to the hotel. Southworth served picnic-style meals to limit time off the field. Catcher Jimmy Wilson expressed the feelings of his teammates when he gave Southworth a new nickname: Billy the Heel.

Breadon made sure the Heel had one foot out the door from season's start. The owner was satisfied when the Cardinals played through their dislike of Southworth into first place early in the season as centerfielder Tayler Douthit outhit nearly every teammate, finished the season with a .416 on-base percentage, and supplemented the typically tremendous production of Frisch, Bottomley, and Hafey. But the failure of every starting pitcher who had led the team to pennants in 1926 and 1928 destroyed the momentum. St. Louis suffered an epic collapse before and after Independence Day. The club lost twenty-two of twenty-seven, allowing eight runs per game in the process to fall into fourth place. Soon Breadon swapped Southworth and McKechnie again. But the die was cast. The Cardinals performed better under the latter but were irretrievably buried in the standings.

McKechnie grew weary of Breadon's whims. So, when the latter offered him a one-year contract after the season, he declined, instead running for tax collector in his hometown of Wilkinsburg, Pennsylvania. Despite the support of Rickey, who arrived there to endorse him, McKechnie lost the election. And rather than beg Breadon for his job back, he signed a four-year deal to manage the pathetic Boston Braves. He briefly turned that franchise around but gained far greater success during a run as skipper of Cincinnati that resulted in a 1940 World Series title and eventual Hall of Fame induction.

Few, however, were lambasting Breadon for personnel decisions in the early 1930s. As the Great Depression began ravaging the nation, the Cardinals launched perhaps the greatest and most entertaining era in franchise history.

CHAPTER SEVEN

The Gas House Gang

INSTABILITY IN THE MANAGERIAL POSITION IS GENERALLY A PRODUCT of losing. Such was not the case in St. Louis in the late 1920s. The revolving door spun by owner Sam Breadon had managers coming and going annually. Number six was first-time skipper Gabby Street, who had served as a coach under Billy Southworth and Bill McKechnie in 1929. But Breadon had finally found his man. The revolving door stopped spinning after Street took over in 1930—at least for a few years.

The former army sergeant, who had fought in several of the fiercest battles in World War I and suffered a puncture wound in his right leg from German airplane fire, appreciated the level of talent he had taken over and felt no need to overmanage. St. Louis had built a powerful lineup capable of outscoring any team in the sport and featured a capable, veteran pitching staff.

In an era of explosive hitting in baseball, the Cardinals were the best outside of Yankee Stadium. Jim Bottomley, Frankie Frisch, Chick Hafey, and Tayler Douthit had either peaked or were entering their prime. Rookie George Watkins exploded onto the scene as well in 1930. Every starting player batted at least .304. The result was a modern franchise record of 1,004 runs scored. The rotation featured no ace but boasted depth led by emerging Bill Hallahan and baseball's last legal spit-baller Burleigh Grimes, a shrewd acquisition in an early season deal that sent serviceable starter Fred Frankhouse and fading southpaw Bill Sherdel to the Braves.

One wonders if Breadon considered kicking Street to the curb after the club struggled most of the year. They opened the season 6–12, recovered on a long homestand to win seventeen of eighteen and take over first place, then fell under .500. The Cardinals were not exactly establishing themselves as road warriors. They stood in fourth place at 48–49 at the end of July. They needed to make up eleven games in two months to capture a pennant, a virtually impossible task, especially after they remained ten games behind on August 19, with most of the future contests away from home. The Redbirds could not just take off. They had to soar.

And that's what they did. They won five straight from Philadelphia. They twice swept Cincinnati. They won three of four from New York, then swept Brooklyn to assume a lead in the standings they never relinquished. They sent runners flying across the bases in record numbers. They scored fifty-three runs during one four-game stretch, including ten against Pittsburgh to clinch the pennant.

A contrast in managerial stability certainly came into focus when St. Louis battled Philadelphia in the World Series. Connie Mack had concluded his thirtieth year of managing the Athletics and would remarkably remain at the helm for twenty more while Breadon had hired and fired annually. But it's the players who decide winning and losing, and the stars in the St. Louis lineup did not rise to the occasion. Philadelphia pitchers George Earnshaw and Lefty Grove stymied the bats of Frish, Bottomley, and Douthit, who combined to bat .114 with one home run in the series. St. Louis scored just eleven runs in six games—only excellent pitching performances by Hallahan and Haines prevented a sweep.

What is historically considered the Gas House Gang era had begun, but the band had not been formed. The most legendary figure of that colorful team was Hall of Fame pitcher Jay Hanna "Dizzy" Dean, who at the age of twenty was promoted from the Class A Texas League to pitch the final game of the regular season after the pennant had been clinched. Dean had gained quite a reputation for his talent in the minors after compiling a 25–10 record that year—his first as a professional. But he did not arrive on the scene to stay until 1932. Neither did most of the players generally associated with the Gas House Gang.

Dizzy Dean was the face of the Gashouse Gang team of the 1930s, not only as the ace of the pitching staff.
PHOTO COURTESY OF THE BASEBALL HALL OF FAME AND MUSEUM

Two who did play for the 1931 edition were outfielder Pepper Martin and first baseman Ripper Collins. The contributions of the two rookies proved critical when the Cardinals hit forty-four fewer home runs and scored nearly two hundred fewer runs that season than they had in 1930. The club became more dependent on aggressiveness and speed on the bases. But pitching depth with the addition of rookie right-hander Paul Derringer bursting onto the scene carried St. Louis to another pennant. The Cardinals gave up on Derringer too soon, trading him to Cincinnati, where he proved himself a standout, but the 1933 deal returned sparkplug shortstop Leo Durocher, who some believe gave the Gas House Gang its moniker.

The 1931 club dominated wire-to-wire, falling no further than 1.5 games behind in late May, and otherwise leading the pack. A three-game sweep of the contending Giants in mid-July launched a 30–11 run that buried the competition. A revenge match against the Athletics awaited.

Street overplayed his hand by starting Derringer in Game 1. The rookie not only took a pounding by Philadelphia standouts Mickey Cochrane, Al Simmons, and Jimmie Foxx in the opener but got knocked out in the fifth inning in a Game 6 rout. But his poor performances were more than overcome by the efforts of Hallahan and Grimes, who combined to hold their hard-hitting opponents to just five runs in thirty-six innings and win all four of their decisions. Included was a taut 4–2 triumph in Game 7. The thirty-eight-year-old Grimes appeared destined for a complete-game shutout but allowed a walk and two singles that cut the lead to two. Street boldly removed Grimes in favor of Hallahan, who retired Max Bishop on a flyout to clinch the world championship.

"I have just realized the ambition of my life," Street proclaimed. "This is the greatest day of my life. I've always wished I could manage a world's championship ball club, but I didn't think I could do it at my age. Pitching was the turning point. We had the better equipped staff, and we beat a great ball club."[1]

The Cardinals were not even a decent ball club in 1932. Attendance at Sportsman's Park dropped by 60 percent as the nation plunged deeper into the Great Depression. General manager Branch Rickey smartly traded the aging Grimes for superstar slugger Hack Wilson, then stupidly swapped the still-viable future Hall of Famer for outfield prospect Bob Parnham, who never spent a day in the major leagues. Rickey also unloaded Hafey, who had a couple strong seasons left in his bat, for pitching mediocrity Benny Frey. The result was a dramatic hitting and pitching downturn. The emergence of Dean as the staff ace proved the lone saving grace in a miserable year during which the Cardinals hung around the pennant race into early July before fading into oblivion.

Rickey continued to tear the team apart in the offseason. He swapped Bottomley, who also had a few good years left, for scrubs Ownie Carroll and Estel Crabtree. He traded Derringer and solid infielder Sparky Adams for Durocher. He even re-signed Grimes, who was all but cooked. But despite the questionable moves, Rickey felt his organization boasted the replacements who could bring a youthful vitality to the club, a brashness that would become legend in baseball history. And he was right.

Among the young players who in 1933 had formed what would soon be known as the Gas House Gang were Martin, whose .315 batting average led the team; blossoming future Hall of Fame outfielder Joe "Ducky" Medwick, who would exceed 100 RBI in each of the next six seasons and win National League Most Valuable Player honors in 1937; the scrappy Durocher; and the eccentric Dean.

The derivation of the Gas House Gang nickname has been debated for decades. But it is generally accepted that it came from their rough-and-tumble playing style and shabby appearance on the field. "They don't look like a major league ballclub," offered the *New York Sun*. "Their uniforms are

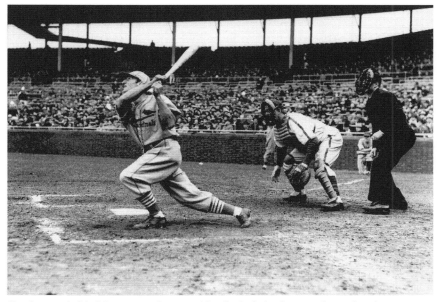

Hard-nosed third baseman Pepper Martin led the league in stolen bases three times during their glory years of the 1930s.
PHOTO COURTESY OF THE BASEBALL HALL OF FAME AND MUSEUM

stained and dirty and patched and ill fitting. . . . They spit out of the sides of their mouths and then wipe the backs of their hands across their shirt fronts. [But] they are not afraid of anybody." One opponent stated, "the Cardinals players usually went into the field unwashed, dirty, and smelly uniforms, which alone spread horror among their rivals."[2]

The actual nickname, however, likely came courtesy of Durocher, who spoke about his new teammates in comparison to those of the more-staid Yankees with whom he once played and their American League brethren. "Why, they wouldn't even let us play in that league over there," he said derisively. He then added in reference to stinky factories that turned coal into gas and were normally placed in the poorest city neighborhoods, "They think we're a bunch of gashousers."[3]

The 1933 Cardinals dropped from contention in late July, motivating Breadon to replace Street at the helm with Frankie Frisch as player-manager. The club responded by winning six consecutive games and performed better down the stretch, but few predicted greatness heading into the next season. St. Louis was pegged as a noncontender in 1934.

The predictions appeared accurate much of the season despite the most potent attack in the National League, which featured a breakout season from Ripper Collins and stunning production from a heretofore mediocrity with the Flintstonian name of Jack Rothrock. Brothers Dizzy and Daffy (Paul) Dean combined with steady Tex Carleton to form a fine pitching trio. The players performed well but spent the first five months trying in vain to win consistently. They hung around the periphery of the pennant race but seemed destined to finish behind the defending champion Giants.

Then it happened. The Redbirds embarked on one of their hottest stretches ever—almost entirely on the road. They took three of four in New York in mid-September, including a doubleheader sweep that attracted 62,573 to the Polo Grounds, to chop their deficit to 3.5 games. The Dean boys performed superbly with the crown on the line. They combined to win twelve of fourteen decisions from September 5 forward, allowing a mere thirteen earned runs in 116 innings pitched between them. They highlighted their streak on September 21 against the host

Dodgers when Dizzy pitched a shutout in the opener, and Paul, not to be outdone, hurled a no-hitter in the nightcap.

The Cardinals, however, needed help. They remained three games behind with just nine left. But Dame Fortune smiled upon them. While they were sweeping Cincinnati to end the regular season, the Giants were losing five straight, including four to lowly Brooklyn and Philadelphia. Some complained that the Cardinals had backed into the pennant. But they had won twenty of twenty-five to finish the year. They also had plenty of momentum heading into the World Series against heavily favored Detroit.

The Tigers were loaded offensively behind Hall of Famers Hank Greenberg, Charlie Gehringer, Goose Goslin, and player-manager Mickey Cochrane. They had scored nearly one thousand runs during the regular season while boasting a team batting average of .300. And the formidable 1–2 pitching punch of Schoolboy Rowe and Tommy Bridges, who had begun his three-year ascension, promised to challenge St. Louis hitters. The Redbords hoped the Dean brothers would outperform the Detroit co-aces and that their superior depth on the mound would play a positive role in the outcome.

Not that they were intimidated. Gas House Gang spiritual leader Dizzy Dean predicted that his team would tame the Tigers in a four-game sweep. Brashness and bravado were common among his teammates. And they played with passion in trying to prove their disdain for the opposition. "The Gas House Gang was the greatest baseball club I ever saw," said Cardinals infielder Burgess Whitehead. "They thought they could beat any ballclub . . . when they got on that ballfield, they played baseball, and they played it to the hilt too. When they did, they slid hard. There was no good fellowship between them and the opposition."[4]

Dizzy put his arm where his mouth was. Cochrane erred by starting late-season pickup General Crowder over Rowe in the opener, and it cost him, though a slew of Detroit errors contributed greatly to a St. Louis rout that featured a four-hit game by Medwick that included a home run. But the Cardinals could not take the momentum and run with it. They fell to the brink of defeat when Bridges, pitching on just one day's rest, outdueled Dizzy in Game 5 before a crowd exceeding thirty-eight thousand at Sportsman's Park. Detroit led the series 3–2 as the teams headed back to Navin Field.

Dizzy's brother came to the rescue. Paul allowed just one earned run in a taut complete-game victory. With 44,551 fans (a veritable throng during the height of the Depression) screaming with anticipation, the younger Dean retired Greenberg on a foul pop to kill a rally in the eighth inning and finished with a flourish for a 4–3 victory that gave Dizzy a chance to clinch the crown the following afternoon. It seemed the die was cast. Cochrane complained that the umpires stole Game 6 from the Tigers. And with Dizzy slated to pitch the clincher most believed Detroit was doomed. And they were right.

Cochrane had started Bridges and Rowe the previous two days. He decided against pitching the former on one day's rest again, opting instead for young right-hander Elden Auker. It was no contest. While Dean mowed down the Tigers in route to a complete-game shutout Frisch launched a seven-run explosion in the third inning with a bases-loaded double. Cochrane desperately summoned Rowe and Bridges from the bullpen to stem the tide but to no avail. The Cardinals rocked them as well.

Living up to their growing reputation as dirty not just in appearance but in the realm of sportsmanship, the Gas House Gang rubbed salt in the Tigers' wounds in the sixth inning when Medwick knocked third baseman Marv Owen to the ground with an aggressive slide, setting off a brief brawl between the two. The Cardinals had already rankled their beaten foe with mocking catcalls from the dugout.

The angry fans showered Medwick with anything they could throw—bottles, fruit, scorecards—when he returned to the outfield in the bottom of the inning. The grounds crew could not keep up. Every time they completed picking up the debris, the fans tossed out more. Cochrane bolted to the scene and vainly begged the fans to calm down. Seated near the St. Louis dugout, alarmed baseball commissioner Kenesaw Mountain Landis called upon Medwick to quell the uprising by shaking Owen's hand under the threat of a Cardinal forfeit. An announcement on the field claimed that the Tigers would be forced to forfeit if the fans could not restrain themselves—a hollow threat given the lopsided score.

The feisty Medwick, who had already been kicked out of the game, had no choice. He reached his hand out to Owen, who rejected the gesture, turned his back, and returned to his position. Medwick then put his protest into action. He fired his glove to the ground and stormed into the dugout.

Joe "Ducky" Medwick managed one of the greatest seasons in baseball history in 1937 to land the National League MVP award.
PHOTO COURTESY OF THE BASEBALL HALL OF FAME AND MUSEUM

More importantly than the inevitable Cardinals triumph by that time, the sport of baseball had delivered entertainment to the beleaguered people of St. Louis and Detroit and captured the attention and passion of Depression-riddled America. Offered the *Sporting News*:

> *The stirring events that brought to a close the 1934 playing season established the game still more firmly as the national sport—first in the hearts of the American people—a dashing, vivid, pulsating, brilliant and clean sport, representative of the American spirit. . . . The St. Louis Cardinals and Detroit Tigers have paved the way for the building up of a new courage among the people of the nation by their example and have lifted baseball to a new pinnacle, where it proudly stands as a symbol of a country that never yields to odds.*[5]

The new world champions had strengthened the sport in its claim as the national pastime as much through their personalities as their play on the field. The "Gas House Gang" moniker became widely embraced in 1935 with Dizzy Dean, who had won National League Most Valuable Player honors the year before, as their undisputed leader. But the strength of his personality also resulted in negative consequences and alienated opponents and teammates. Among many examples occurred after a three-inning stint on the mound against the still-seething Giants during spring training 1935. Dean meandered over to the New York dugout and asked if anyone could cash a check for $5,300—the winner's share from the 1934 World Series. He mocked their five-game losing streak to end of the previous season by stating, "I wanna thank you fellas for collapsin' so we could make all that dough."[6]

It seemed the more success and confidence with which Dizzy was imbued, the more intolerable he became. And the more Paul followed along. Both proved not only their massive egos but short tempers. It was a deadly combination for opposing batters bold enough to actually touch them up for hits and runs. During one poor performance against the Phillies the elder Dean threw at the head of one batter and brushed another back. Phillies catcher Jimmie Wilson, once a teammate and close friend of Dean, complained, "It's getting so you can't get a base hit off those Deans without getting beaned your next time up. They think they can get away with anything, but by God, the Phils have declared war on them." Dean's dismissive reply: "You can tell that Wilson he can kiss my ass. Them Phillies can't hurt anybody. None of 'em can hit a lick."[7]

Teammates were not immune to his temper that sometimes resulted in childish behavior. During one game at Forbes Field in Pittsburgh, he grew so incensed at an error by second baseman Burgess Whitehead that led to four unearned runs and the loss of a 2–0 lead that he intentionally began lobbing balls to the plate for the Pirates to slaughter. A verbal battle between Dizzy and Collins ensued, with Daffy and Medwick joining. Martin was forced to cool his hot teammates before they became physical. Frisch allowed Dean to remain in the game through six innings while the Bucs rapped line drives all over the ballpark and tallied nine runs.

The manager did threaten to fine Dizzy five grand and suspend him if he ever again failed to pitch his best. Dean reacted petulantly, asking for a trade, then throwing a shot to Ducky. "I'm not goin' to stand for this stuff," he insisted. "As for Medwick, I'll crack him on his Hungarian beezer."[8]

St. Louis fans were not as lenient as Frisch. A crowd estimated at 14,500 at Sportsman's Park showered Dean with boos when he arrived at the plate for his first at-bat during his next start. Some pelted him with lemons from the upper deck. His teammates took the pressure off by scoring in every inning and slamming twenty-one hits as Dean cruised to a complete-game victory.

That game proved far more typical of his performance in 1935 than that in Pittsburgh. Dean got away with his abrasiveness as the unquestioned leader of the Gas House Gang because he was their best player—at least during his peak. He concluded that season with a 28–12 record and 3.04 ERA. He combined with Paul to win forty-seven games while Collins, Martin, and Medwick continued to rake.

The Cardinals won ninety-six games that year, to exceed their total from their world championship season, but they finished in second place behind Chicago. They battled back into the race by winning eighteen of nineteen to start July after falling 9.5 games behind and even forged ahead by blitzing the National League on a 29–8 run into early September. They continued to perform well, but a Cubs' epic twenty-one-game winning streak decided the race. Among those victories was a three-game sweep of St. Louis.

Soon Daffy faded, then Dizzy followed suit as bursitis ravaged his arm. The Gas House Gang faded into memory. But eventually, as hundreds of major league players battled far more dangerous enemies overseas than their opponents on the baseball field, the Redbirds rose again.

CHAPTER EIGHT

The Prewar Years

DIZZY AND DAFFY DEAN WERE NOT INTERESTED IN SITTING AT HOME and resting their weary arms during the off-season. They considered themselves entertainers. So, they served as star attractions in barnstorming tours that traveled throughout the country. While segregation shamefully remained prominent in many cities in which they played and in major league baseball itself, the two St. Louis stars performed against Negro League teams such as the Kansas City Monarchs (featuring immortal pitcher Satchel Paige) and the Pittsburgh Crawfords.

The motivation was more monetary than humanitarian, especially considering the Great Depression continued to devastate the nation. The Deans earned more money barnstorming than they did cashing paychecks from the Cardinals. The tour stopped for daily games. Travel took a toll on their bodies. Pitchers risked arm injuries that could destroy their careers. But ownership understood they could not stop their players from making money on the side playing ball.

After all, Dizzy and Daffy were stars. They even earned $5,000 a week performing in vaudeville shows on Broadway—the former as a fast-talker and the latter as a straight man. They worked with Shemp Howard of Three Stooges fame in a film titled *Farmers*. But the hectic schedule on the diamonds ended both their careers prematurely. That of Paul was thoroughly destroyed. He first felt soreness in his right arm during a barnstorming game in Des Moines, though from a slip while warming up in the outfield rather than on the mound. His aching wing proved so worrisome that he sat out some games and even tossed the

The Brothers Dean—Dizzy and Daffy—shook things up for opposing batters and the organization during their tumultuous time with the Cardinals.
PHOTO COURTESY OF THE BASEBALL HALL OF FAME AND MUSEUM

ball underhand in others. Soon Breadon ordered the younger Dean to leave the tour.

Dizzy convinced him that both should stage holdouts for bigger bucks before the 1935 season, but the effort largely failed. He asked for $25,000 and still landed the heftiest contract for any National League pitcher at $18,500. The club gave Paul far less respect. He was barely offered half of what he requested and was forced to sign for $8,500.

The pair continued to express a spirit of rebelliousness that threatened physical violence and reflected on their selfishness and family bond rather than love of team and teammates. After walking three batters in the third inning of a losing battle in Brooklyn on May 8, 1935, Paul started a verbal altercation with umpire Dolly Stark. The pitcher grew so angry that he petulantly stomped off the mound. "Gee whillikins," he said later, "I wished I had a hun'red thousand dollars. I'd walk right up to Stark and punch him square in the nose. . . . Then I'd do the same to [fellow umpire Cy) Rigler. But I ain't got the hun'red grand." Offered Dizzy: "Okay, Paul. We'll save up our money, get the hundred grand, and then we'll both punch 'em in the nose."[1]

Soon the only Dean worth much of anything was Dizzy. After his second consecutive nineteenth-win season in 1935, Paul threatened to remain on his farm throughout the year if not offered the $15,000 deal he asked for the previous year. Breadon sent him another contract for $8,500, prompting him and Dizzy to launch personal boycotts of spring training. The plan worked. Dizzy signed for $22,800 and Daffy for $12,000.

The holdout, however, wreaked havoc with Paul physically. He had gained fifty pounds in the offseason that he did not work off. He arrived out of shape the day before the Cardinals left Florida. Yet he pitched a complete game in his first start and performed well into early June. Then his season and career quickly collapsed. Pain in his right shoulder proved to be torn cartilage. He pitched only sporadically the rest of the year and was never the same. Daffy not only failed to win another game in 1935, but he lost his enthusiasm for the sport. He made just seven starts for St. Louis from 1937 to 1939 and finished his career as a little-used journeyman.

His older brother did not even last that long in a Cardinals uniform. He managed one more excellent season, carrying a suddenly woeful pitching staff on his shoulders in 1936 with a 24–13 record and a 3.17 ERA. But his antics—particularly the holdouts—grew tiresome to Breadon. Rickey, who embraced the philosophy of trading players just before a perceived deterioration, tried to time his swap of Dizzy accordingly. He sent Dean to the Cubs for pitchers Curt Davis and Clyde Shoun and outfielder Tuck Stainback. Only Davis, who earned thirty-four victories in two strong seasons, contributed positively as the Cardinals tried to overcome the loss of their ace. But Dizzy faded as only a spot starter in the Windy City.

The departures of the Dean brothers essentially ended the Gas House Gang era, though some believe it had already started dissipating when the nickname itself began to stick in 1935. The period certainly ended when the two rambunctious pitchers left despite the presence of some of its other personalities, including Frisch, Martin, Medwick, and Durocher. More impactful was the inability of Rickey to replace the pitching production of the Deans. The Cardinals continued to hit—young slugger Johnny Mize had in 1936 replaced Collins at first base and embarked on a Hall of Fame career, and two years later outfielder Enos "Country" Slaughter had arrived to launch a long run of greatness that landed him in Cooperstown as well. But by that time, the rotation had deteriorated into one of the worst in the National League.

Something had to give. Breadon, who had learned a valuable lesson about continuity after his period of spinning a revolving door of managers, would have preferred to keep both Rickey and Frisch. But the relationship between the general manager and the feisty skipper had become untenable. The two clashed about personnel decisions. Breadon did not want to lose Rickey and figured managers were easier to replace. The owner understood that the Cubs were eyeing the GM who had built the Gas House Gang into a World Series champion.

The writing was on the wall. Cardinal players began to suspect toward the end of the 1938 season that Frisch's days were numbered. "My guess is that Frisch wanted to play certain players, and Rickey wanted him to play somebody else," offered third baseman Don Gutteridge years later.[2]

Frisch felt the pressure. Heading into the last month of the season, he confronted Breadon, for whom he conveyed great respect, after hearing reports of his professional demise. Frisch wanted to learn of his fate immediately so he could seek employment elsewhere for the following season. Reports circulated that Breadon offered to keep him only if he accepted a cut in salary. No dice. Breadon canned Frisch before the September 11 game against Pittsburgh. The *Sporting News* reported that an emotional Breadon "put his arms around Frankie, bade him goodbye and there was mist in his eyes when he turned quickly and hustled out of the room."[3]

The Redbirds responded to replacement Mike Gonzalez, a Cuban who made history as the first Latin American manager in major league baseball, by winning six straight. But they collapsed down the stretch and finished with their worst record since 1924. He was not long for the job—Breadon promoted Ray Blades from minor league Rochester to take over in 1939.

The owner believed rightfully that his team boasted far too much talent to finish under .500 but that the pitching staff had been poorly utilized. Blades arrived with a different philosophy that fit more appropriately in twenty-first-century baseball than in the 1930s and 1940s. He eschewed the notion that starters needed to finish games. Blades brought in relievers willy-nilly based on matchups, which, in turn, gave everyone on the staff a feeling of involvement. And he had the talent to make it work. The 1939 Cardinals finished last in the National League with forty-five complete games, which at the time tied the 1920 Phillies for the lowest total in the history of the senior circuit. Yet their 3.59 team ERA placed second to the Reds. Eleven pitchers started for St. Louis that season, and seven pitched at least 146 innings, all of whom compiled ERAs under 3.82. "My idea is never to save anybody for tomorrow. . . . Let's win today's game today," Blades explained. "Save a man for tomorrow and you may lose two games. I'll relieve with anyone who can relieve. . . . There won't be any regular rotation necessarily. In a short series I believe in trying to beat the other club's best pitcher with my best pitcher. And with all my pitchers if necessary."

That success, coupled with a relentless offensive attack, vaulted the Cardinals back into contention. The establishment of young sluggers Slaughter and Mize coupled with Gas House Gang holdover Medwick and flash-in-the-pan outfielder Terry Moore resulted in a juggernaut. The club was a doubles machine, leading the NL with a whopping 332 two-baggers. The team even pushed powerful Cincinnati down the stretch, closing to within 2.5 games of first place before a September 28 loss to the host Reds dashed their dreams of a pennant. But Breadon was impressed. He rewarded Blades with another one-year contract.

Good thing for the owner it wasn't longer. What had been an innovation for Blades turned into an obsession when the team began losing in 1940. He wore out a path to the mound, using eighty-six pitchers in twenty-nine games as 1939 standouts Davis and Mort Cooper went winless. A 6–14 stretch in May and June sent the Cardinals reeling into sixth place and permanently out of the race. Disenchanted St. Louis fans stayed away in droves. Breadon became alarmed when a mere 7,661 fans showed up for a June 2 doubleheader. That motivated the impatient Breadon to fire Blades five days later and eventually replace him with former Cardinals outfielder Billy Southworth, who had also managed the club briefly in 1929. Breadon even bypassed a consultation with Rickey on the canning of Blades. The owner soon wiped out the last vestige of the Gas House Gang by trading Medwick and Davis to the Dodgers for four mediocrities. The swap would have proven disastrous had the Cardinals not boasted the talent to overcome it. Ducky and Davis proved they still had fine years left.

Baseball, however, became far less important in the grand scheme as military production pushed the country out of the Great Depression and the guns of war began blazing in Europe and Asia. The sport proved only a pleasant diversion from the seemingly inevitable drawing of the United States into what would eventually become World War II. The need for manpower overseas wreaked havoc with major league rosters, including that of the Cardinals. But the depth of the franchise allowed it to handle the player shortage far better than its National League brethren. A period of dominance awaited.

Chapter Nine

Winning Battles on the Diamond

Ray Blades was gone, but his philosophy that pitching depth was a key to success lived on as the new decade gathered steam. The Cardinals owned enough arms to handle the unknown—injuries and the loss of hurlers to the war effort. They had plenty of everything, courtesy of a ridiculous thirty-one farm clubs, including two at the highest level that combined to sport a 276–209 record in 1940.

St. Louis simply weathered the storm in the seasons to come. When one pitcher faltered or left to fight overseas, Southworth plugged in a viable replacement. One-hit wonder southpaw Ernie White burst upon the scene to lead the team in wins and ERA in 1941 but faltered thereafter before joining the war effort. Aging right-hander Lon Warneke had performed consistently well for five seasons in earning two All-Star Game berths before fading in 1941. Young right-hander Johnny Beazley exploded onto the scene as a rookie with a 21–6 record and a 2.13 ERA, but he joined the service and remained away for three years, never to pitch at anywhere near that level again. Southpaw Howie Pollett led the league in ERA in 1943 before he, too, was lost to more important battles, then returned in 1946 to achieve the same feat.

The Cardinals did more than survive. They thrived despite every departure, including that of Mize, who continued to slam home runs for the Giants after being traded for three mediocrities four days after the Japanese bombed Pearl Harbor. They earned the distinction as the premier franchise in baseball during the war years after falling just short of the pennant in 1941. They appeared destined to finish behind Brooklyn again in 1942 when they fell ten games back in early August despite the promising performance of rookie outfielder Stan Musial. But they sizzled down the stretch, winning a remarkable forty-three of fifty-one, including five of six against the Dodgers. They arrived at the World Series against the vaunted Yankees as one of the hottest clubs in baseball history.

They took their momentum and ran with it against a New York team still unaffected by the war as standout hitters Joe DiMaggio, Bill Dickey, and Joe Gordon, and Hall of Fame hurler Red Ruffing remained dominant. The Yankees had led the American League in runs scored and team ERA and finished with 103 wins.

But they were no match for the high-flying Redbirds. That is, aside from Game 1, when they led 7–0 and held on. A four-run ninth gave St. Louis momentum it never relinquished. Southworth pushed all the right buttons as his team won one taut game after another. He stuck with Beazley in Game 2 after a three-run Yankees rally tied it in the eighth and the first two batters singled in the ninth. Slaughter nailed a runner at third base with a fine throw from right field before Beazley retired tough-out Phil Rizzuto to end it. Southworth picked young Ernie White to pitch Game 3 before nearly seventy thousand fans at Yankee Stadium and was rewarded with a 2–0 shutout. The manager summoned usual starter Max Lanier to relieve in Game 4 after the Cardinals had blown a 6–1 lead, and he pitched three shutout innings in a 9–6 victory. And Southworth's decision to play rookie third baseman Whitey Kurowski paid off in the clincher at Sportsman's Park when the twenty-four-year-old blasted a game-winning homer in the ninth. The Cardinals were World Series champions. And they had twice beaten a team that had lost just nineteen regular season games at home and a club that had won all eight of its previous Fall Classics.

Though what had now become known as World War II dampened enthusiasm in a rather subdued postgame celebration, Kurowski was particularly jubilant. He playfully rubbed the white hair of baseball commissioner Kenesaw Mountain Landis, who had received a thumbs-up from President Roosevelt when asked after the attack on Pearl Harbor if the season should be played. Kurowski also tore up the hat worn by NL president Ford Frick and led his teammates in a rousing rendition of the silly Spike Jones tune, "Pass the Biscuits, Mirandy," which was embraced as the team's victory song.

Ineligible to join the battles overseas due to an osteomyelitis, an inflammatory bone infection, Kurowski became a mainstay in a lineup decimated by defections to the military and continued to produce in peacetime. The five-time all-star averaged ninety-six RBI and ninety-one runs scored while batting over .300 in three of four seasons from 1944 to 1947. But it was the brilliant Musial who keyed a run of dominance during World War II and beyond. It was no coincidence that the only season from 1942 to 1946 that St. Louis did not win the National League pennant was 1945—the year Musial left to join the navy.

The Cardinals overcame the departures of premier outfielders Slaughter and Moore to blow away the National League competition in 1943 with a twelve-game winning streak in July that allowed them to cruise

Stan Musial, shown here with fellow immortal Mickey Mantle, was simply one of the finest players ever to don a major league uniform.
PHOTO COURTESY OF THE BASEBALL HALL OF FAME AND MUSEUM

to another pennant and a rematch against the revenge-seeking Yankees. But despite the losses to World War II of such standouts as DiMaggio and Ruffing, the Yankees indeed exacted retribution. The loss of Slaughter and Moore finally caught up with the Cardinals. They performed poorly in the clutch throughout, managing just three hits in twenty at-bats with runners in scoring position over the last three games, including a 0-for-9 disaster in a 2–0 Game 5 defeat that ended the series.

Some believed that as the war drew more major league players in, it would become the great equalizer. It did not in the National League. The Cardinals continued to quickly turn its pennant races into a farce. They forged ahead in early April 1944 and never looked back. They threatened to win 120 games after a 41–8 run raised their record to a ridiculous 89–29, but a poor September stretch with little motivation to win resulted in a 105–49–3 mark and crosstown showdown against the surprising St. Louis Browns in what became known as the Trolley World Series. No need to travel—every game was played at Sportsman's Park.

The event turned into the Mort Cooper Show. Coming off his third-consecutive twenty-win season, he performed well in a 2–1 defeat in the opener before hurling a critical shutout in Game 5 with twelve strike-outs to place his team within one game of the championship. Pitching mates Max Lanier and Ted Wilks, who had won seventeen of twenty-one decisions as a rookie starter before spending most of his career in the bull-pen, combined to finish the job in a 3–1 victory. The Cardinals' pitching benefited from a balanced attack throughout as nearly every hitter in the lineup contributed to a win.

The most significant difference was defense. The Browns committed ten errors in the series to just one for their opponent. The vital shortstop position spotlighted the gap in performance. Browns shortstop Vern Stephens (known as "Pop-up Stephens" for his penchant to hit sky-high pops at the plate) committed three errors, while blossoming Cardinals counterpart Marty Marion fielded twenty-seven plays flawlessly. Teammates and the media marveled at the human vacuum cleaner.

"The best ballplayer in the series was Marty Marion," said Frick. "He showed us some shortstopping we've rarely seen before and won't see many times again. He killed off at least four big Brown rallies. They found it just about impossible to hit one past him." Added Hall of Fame manager Connie Mack, who at age eighty-one was still managing the Athletics, "I've looked at a lot of shortstops in my day, but that fellow is the best I've ever seen."[1]

Marion had been wowing the baseball world since 1940. His contributions to the Cardinals did not go unappreciated despite limited production with the bat. He earned National League Most Valuable Player honors in 1944 despite wholly mediocre offensive numbers that included a .267 batting average, six home runs, fifty-three RBI, and fifty runs scored. One could claim those statistics as the worst of any MVP in baseball history, but in citing modern analytics, his 3.6 defensive WAR that season was the best of his career.

The Cardinals were again world champions, but storm clouds were gathering around opening day in 1945. As the Allies were on the verge of defeating Hitler and Nazi Germany, batterymate brothers Mort and Walker Cooper were engaging in an albeit far less important battle against penny-pinching team owner, Sam Breadon. The Coopers staged a strike and threatened to boycott the first series of the season against the Cubs in Chicago. Mort had inked a $12,000 contract for that year after the owner claimed that the federal Wage Stabilization Act of 1943 prevented him from paying any player more than what the highest-paid teammate had earned in 1942. Breadon contended that since Moore earned twelve grand that year, he could not offer another penny to Mort Cooper. But the pitcher soon learned that Breadon had indeed given Marion more. So, Walker left camp and stated that they would not return until Mort received a salary offer of at least $15,000.

The Coopers did not make good on their threat. They returned for Opening Day but did not remain with the team for long. A month after Walker was inducted into the army as the Americans made their final push in the Pacific, Mort was dispatched to the Boston Braves for pitcher Red Barrett and $60,000. It seemed like a dead giveaway—Cooper was off to a brilliant start, and Barrett's career had been marked by mediocrity. Cooper blanked the Reds in his first start and continued to pitch well. But the elbow problem that had plagued him earlier in his career reemerged, forcing an operation in August. Cooper returned for a decent 1946 but was never the same.

Meanwhile, Barrett gave the Cardinals one tremendous season upon his arrival. He compiled a 21–9 record, led the NL in innings pitched, and finished third in the MVP balloting before returning to his previous mediocrity. The Cooper controversy took a toll on the team the first two months. In proving that early games count just as much as those in September, the Cardinals simply fell too far behind to catch up to the Cubs. They dropped 7.5 games back in late May before hitting their stride. They remained on the fringe of the pennant race until sweeping a three-game series against the Cubs at Wrigley Field before 112,000 fans just before Labor Day. The Cardinals chopped the deficit to 1.5 games late in September and continued to play well down the stretch, but a five-game Chicago winning streak dashed their hopes of another pennant.

A defeat of Cincinnati to close that campaign was the last for Southworth as St. Louis skipper. He signed a far more lucrative offer to manage the Braves, which he transformed into a winner and 1948 National League champion. Southworth was replaced by friendly and outgoing Eddie Dyer, who had become familiar with the younger players as a minor league manager.

Every major league team welcomed back significant talent from the war in 1946, but few could embrace the return of better players than Musial and Slaughter. The pair proved they had lost none of their skills. The former had still not hit his stride as a power hitter but remained an extra-base machine. Musial led the National League in batting average (.365), doubles (50), and triples (20) in earning his second MVP in four years. Slaughter paced the senior circuit with a career-high 130 RBI to finish third in the same voting. Given Kurowski's continued production, it was no wonder St. Louis led the league in runs scored.

Their offensive brilliance would have gone to waste if not for lithe left-hander Howie Pollet, who returned to action after helping entertain troops in the Pacific with baseball exhibitions to serve as the team's lone consistent winning starting pitcher in 1946. Pollet won one critical contest after another as the Cardinals, after a slow start, heated up to battle

Brooklyn tooth-and-nail down the stretch. But he lost badly in his final two outings as the offense shut down as well. That allowed the Dodgers to forge a tie for the crown and force a best-of-three playoff for the pennant—the first in major league history.

That's when Pollet rose to the occasion again. He hurled a complete game for a 4–2 win in an opener that featured two players, one of whom became more famous for his failures five years later and another who gained greater notoriety in a future endeavor. Pollet defeated right-hander Ralph Branca, who in 1951 surrendered the "Shot Heard 'Round the World" home run to Giants hitter Bobby Thomson that lost the pennant for the Dodgers. And the offensive hero in the St. Louis victory that day was rookie catcher Joe Garagiola, who made his name decades later in television on the Saturday Game of the Week and various game shows. Garagiola slammed three singles and drove in two critical runs in Game 1 to play the role of offensive hero.

Right-hander Murry Dickson, who had pitched mostly in relief during the regular season, matched Pollet pitch-for-pitch in Game 2 at Ebbets Field in the first televised game in major league history. The Cardinals continued to wreck Brooklyn pitching without hitting a home run. Their thirteen hits raised their total to twenty-seven in the playoffs as they stretched their lead to 8–1 in the ninth inning before the Dodgers threw a scare into their opponent and its fans by scoring three runs and loading the bases in the bottom of the inning. But after allowing a single and walk to exacerbate the mess, usual starter Harry "The Cat" Brecheen fanned tough-out Eddie Stanky, who had led the National League in on-base percentage, and Howie Schultz to clinch the victory and pennant.

Ted Williams and the Red Sox awaited in the World Series. Impatient Boston manager Joe Cronin had railed against the three-game playoff format in major league baseball that had forced his players to cool their heels and even play an exhibition game to remain mentally focused and physically prepared. Cronin, who called in vain for the sport to reduce such showdowns to one game, grew more perturbed when the Splendid Splinter hurt his elbow on a hit-by-pitch in the meaningless contest. "If Brooklyn and St. Louis weren't going through best-of-three playoffs this week, we wouldn't have had to play any exhibition games to keep in trim," Cronin complained. "And if there had been no exhibition games, Ted would not have been hurt needlessly."[2]

Ted would soon be hurt again by what was then a revolutionary shift first utilized against him by Indians manager Lou Boudreau that summer. Williams managed five measly singles in the seven-game series. Dyer claimed upon its conclusion that the shift featuring three infielders on the right side of second base robbed the slugger of at least three more hits.

The result was dramatic. The impotence of Williams played a significant role in his team scoring just twenty runs. But it was not Pollet who emerged as mound hero. Rather, it was Brecheen who became the first major league pitcher to win three decisions in a seven-game series, including the critical last two games. A sellout crowd at Sportsman's Park watched Brecheen, who managed just a 15–15 record in the regular season, hurl a complete game in a 4–1 victory in Game 6 that kept his team alive. Another throng at the same venue witnessed with joy as Brecheen pitched two shutout innings to close out a taut 4–3 win that clinched the series.

But it was the aggressive baserunning of Slaughter in the bottom of the eighth that made the difference. He ran through the stop sign at third to score the winning run from first on a Harry Walker double, when Boston shortstop Johnny Pesky, who admitted after the game he was shocked when Slaughter tried to score, hesitated on his relay throw home.

"When the ball went into left-center," Slaughter explained, "I hit second base, and I said to myself, 'I can score.' I didn't know whether the ball had been cut off or not. I didn't know nothin'. It was a gutsy play. But, you know, two men out and the winning run, you can't let the grass grow under your feet."[3]

What was among the most exciting events in baseball history ended dramatically after Brecheen allowed back-to-back singles to open the ninth. With runners on first and third and one out, he retired backup catcher Roy Partee and pinch-hitter Tom McBride. The final out came with a scare. The McBride grounder hit a rock in the infield and ran up the arm of St. Louis second baseman and future manager Red Schoendienst, who trapped it against his body and flipped it to Marion. The Redbirds had won their third world championship in five years.

This time the fans could celebrate a crown without fretting events overseas. The club had exceeded one million in attendance that year for the first time in its history. The players targeted the hero. They mobbed Brecheen. Kurowski and catcher Del Rice hoisted him upon their shoulders. Delirious fans tossed seat cushions onto the field. Office workers in the streets of St. Louis tossed toilet-paper streamers out their windows and launched a spontaneous parade. Fans leaving Sportsman's Park soon joined the players celebrating on the field. Even umpire Charlie Berry got into the act. He tried to snatch Brecheen's glove for a keepsake, but pitcher Red Barrett grabbed Berry's hand to prevent the theft.

The Cardinals eventually escaped into the confines of their locker room for a private celebration. And quite the raucous party it was. They drank beer (champagne had apparently yet to be accepted as the celebratory drink of choice), posed for pictures, and sang songs such as "A Hot Time in the Old Town Tonight" and the traditional "Pass the Biscuits, Mirandy," with team trainer Doc Weaver spinning the records. The tightwad Breadon felt so thankful for Dyer's performance as a rookie pilot that he added a $5,000 bonus to his $13,000 salary for winning it all.

The sterling reputation of the Cardinals that had peaked in 1946 did not last. But it had little to do with their performance on the field the following year, despite a horrible 20–28 start that even the successful return of the hot-hitting Medwick in his career swan song did not help. More troubling—certainly from a historical perspective—was their treatment of baseball pioneer Jackie Robinson when the club played Brooklyn in 1947. St. Louis players, particularly Southerners such as Slaughter, unmercifully taunted the soon-to-be Rookie of the Year who bravely integrated the sport. Moreover, Breadon visited New York ostensibly to join the team in Brooklyn and discuss with players the possibility of firing Dyer, but in reality he received a stern warning from NL president Ford Frick that an alleged players strike against Robinson proposed by St. Louis players would result in suspensions.

Dyer strongly denied that his players threatened a strike against the brave rookie. Frick revealed that Breadon had shared the rumor with him in claiming that his players were simply "letting off a little steam." Whether the Cardinals or any other team actually planned to refuse to play has never been confirmed. The prevailing belief is that the players talked about it but never followed through and that Dyer knew nothing about it. In fact, Robinson once described his first trip to St. Louis with fondness for the manager. "I had serious misgivings about what was going to happen in St. Louis," Robinson said after the 1947 season. "Then a wonderful thing happened. When I walked out onto the field, Dyer got up from the bench and shook my hand. He welcomed me to St. Louis and the big leagues. I'll never forget some of the things he said in that quiet moment. It lifted some of the load from my shoulders."[4]

The load off Dyer's shoulders was lifted when the Cardinals embarked on a nine-game winning streak during a long homestand in May and zoomed back into the pennant race. They pulled within five games of the first-place Dodgers, but a series defeat at Sportsman's Park to that team followed by a four-game sweep at home against the Giants destroyed their chances at another crown.

That proved to be Breadon's last chance at a championship as well. He stunned the city and the baseball world by selling the team to businessman Fred Saigh and former postmaster general and University of St. Louis athletic standout Bob Hannegan. The now-silver-haired Breadon was visibly shaken and unhappy when he announced the sale in November. Hannegan purchased the franchise for an estimated $3.5 million, the largest sum ever at the time for a major league club. On that fateful November day after he had completed the sale, the seventy-two-year-old could only sputter out, "Every day, I am less sufficient, and at my age it's time to quit." Eighteen months later, he died of cancer, and his ashes were scattered over the Mississippi River.[5]

A new era of St. Louis baseball had begun. But competitively it was not much different than the old one. The Cardinals remained a contender. Their stars continued to shine. And none shone brighter than Musial.

CHAPTER TEN

Stan the Man

THE EARNING OF "LEGEND" AMONG BASEBALL GREATS IS OFTEN NOT limited to talent and production alone. Some also gain fame with the flair with which they play the game. Many strengthen their stardom through either positive or negative interaction with the fans and media. Others hype themselves intentionally or unintentionally through their lifestyles.

Not Stan Musial. He performed rather blandly. His passion for the sport was never displayed externally but rather felt internally. He rarely made headlines for anything he did away from the diamond. All he did was post numbers that ranked him among the best ever to don a major league uniform. Perhaps his simple greatness was described best by broadcasting legend Bob Costas, who compared Musial to superstar contemporaries as Ted Williams, Joe DiMaggio, and Willie Mays.

"He didn't hit a homer in his last at-bat; he hit a single," Costas said. "He didn't hit in fifty-six straight games. He married his high school sweetheart and stayed married to her, never married a Marilyn Monroe. He didn't play with the sheer joy and style that goes alongside Willie Mays's name. None of those easy things are there to associate with Stan Musial. All Musial represents is more than two decades of sustained excellence and complete decency as a human being."[1]

Even his nickname was simpler and more succinct. In the era of Splendid Splinters, Joltin' Joes, and Say Hey Kids, he was known plainly as Stan the Man. It was a nickname admirably given to him by Dodgers fans, who chanted, "Here comes that man," after Musial continued to

Few players in major league history have made as great an impact on their franchise than Stan "The Man" Musial.
PHOTO COURTESY OF THE BASEBALL HALL OF FAME AND MUSEUM

wear out Brooklyn pitchers at Ebbets Field, and coined officially by *St. Louis Post-Dispatch* writer Bob Broeg.[2]

While debates raged about the respective merits of Williams and DiMaggio in the American League, no arguments were waged about the best darn hitter in the National League—at least until the likes of Mays and Hank Aaron arrived. It was Musial. How could anyone claim otherwise as he hit over .300 in seventeen consecutive seasons and led the NL in batting average seven times while winning three Most Valuable Player in his first six full years?

The son of a Polish immigrant father and second-generation Czechoslovakian mother, Stanislaus Francis Musial was born on November 21, 1920. His passion for and focus on athletics growing up in the sports hotbed around the steel mills and zinc mines of western Pennsylvania resulted in mediocrity in the classroom and greatness in both baseball and basketball. Despite his average grades, the young Musial was a popular student embraced for his friendliness and easygoing nature.

His father, Lukasz, struggled to make ends meet during the Great Depression, loading bales of wire into freight cars for the American Steel and Wire Company, which eventually led to a severe bout with alcoholism. His mother, Mary, toiled as a domestic worker. The family often depended on donations from food pantries to survive. Lukasz expected his sons to quit high school before graduation to supplement income by working in the mines as well. But Stan yearned to complete his education, greatly for his love of playing baseball. Mary supported that desire, even piecing together material to create makeshift baseballs for him. Stan did help out by taking odd jobs, but he remained at Donora High School.

The youth became so adept at the sport he loved that he spurned a basketball scholarship offer from the University of Pittsburgh to sign with the Cardinals in 1937. He later claimed regret at foregoing college to sign with St. Louis for $65 a month. But he never bemoaned hooking up with the franchise with which he remained for nearly three decades. Musial offered the following about that decision in his autobiography:

What made me sign with the Cardinals? Because they used salesmanship, the personal touch. Where others wrote, they talked. Where others waited, they acted. That early bird that got the worm must have been a Redbird.[3]

Musial began his minor league stint as a pitcher while also finishing up his high school career. Given the choice to compete for Williamson (West Virginia) or fellow Class D club Greensburg (Pennsylvania), he chose the former so he could play for manager Ollie Vanek, who had signed him as a scout, never mind that it was farther from home. But after one season, it appeared possible he might return to Donora to stay. He performed poorly on the mound and at the plate. He soon he began to display the talent, work ethic, and dedication that defined his career. He worked tirelessly, perfecting what became revered as one of the sweetest swings in the sport.

Musial as a Hall of Fame player quickly began to surface. He had yet to give up on pitching in 1939, but despite sporting a 9–2 mark in 1939, his walk total remained inordinately high, and his .352 batting average pointed to a career as a hitter. Under the tutelage of Daytona Beach manager Dickie Kerr, whose claim to fame was winning two games in the

1919 World Series for the notorious Black Sox, his career sprang to life in 1940 after having overcome the disappointment of his first demotion. Musial even appeared destined to finally flourish on the mound after marrying Lillian, his high school sweetheart to whom he would remain wed for seventy-one years. The left-hander finished 18–5 that season, with a 2.62 ERA. But his wildness remained pronounced, and he continued to show promise with the bat.

Any decision about his future position ended on August 11, when he dove for a sinking liner while manning center field in the second game of a doubleheader. He crashed onto his shoulder and felt immediate pain. The injury not only cost him twenty games but his pitching career as well. Even as an outfielder for a quarter century in the major leagues, his arm never recovered, and the injury prevented him from become a five-tool player.

Musial returned from the injury and learned the hard way that he would never return to the mound. He even considered giving up baseball and leaving for home to work in the steel mills. But Kerr talked him out of it. "This is a great game, and you can still make it," he advised. "As a pitcher, no. But the way you can hit, the managers in the upper leagues wouldn't fool around with you as a pitcher anyway. They'd want you in there every day, instead of every fourth game. This is a great game; you won't be happy out of it."[4]

Four tools were plenty for Musial, especially given his penchant for spraying line drives all over the field. He never hit more than thirty-nine home runs in a season but emerged as the premier extra-base threat in baseball and still finished his career with 475 homers. His severe crouch at the plate with back turned to the pitcher allowed him to uncoil as he unleashed his swing, creating greater bat speed and hitting the ball harder than nearly all his contemporaries. "He could hit .300 with a fountain pen," quipped Cardinals catcher and longtime broadcaster Joe Garagiola. Offered legendary baseball announcer Vin Scully, "How good was Stan Musial? Good enough to take your breath away."[5]

The iconic Musial stance was brushed off by some as unsustainable. But by 1941 it had become apparent that it could drive him to stardom. He skyrocketed through the St. Louis system with eye-popping numbers as he could now focus entirely on his jobs at the plate and in the outfield. He jumped from Class C Springfield to Double-A Rochester before debuting with the Cardinals on September 17. He proved undaunted by the rapid rise that would have overwhelmed most rookies upon their arrival. Musial batted .462 down the stretch in the heat of a pennant race and struck out just once in forty-seven at-bats. His brilliance led St. Louis teammates to wonder why he had not been promoted earlier. If he had, perhaps their team would have caught the Dodgers and snagged the crown.

Mize and others even theorized that Cardinals management preferred to remain in the race but fall short of a pennant for financial reasons. Why else, he asked, would they not promote Musial after budding star Enos Slaughter injured his shoulder in a game against Pittsburgh on August 10? "Here we're fighting the Dodgers for a pennant, [and Rickey] said we didn't have anybody in the minor leagues to help us," Mize recalled. "Then in September he brings up Musial. Why didn't he bring Musial up earlier? That's what all the platers wanted to know. We'd have gone ahead and won the pennant. I'll tell you what the talk used to be about Rickey. Stay in the pennant race until the last week of the season, then get beat. . . . That way he drew the crowds all year, and then later on, the players couldn't come in for the big raise for winning the pennant and maybe the World Series. I don't know if it's true or not, but that was the talk."[6]

The six National League crowns and four Fall Classic triumphs earned by St. Louis during Rickey's stint as GM speaks volumes against that notion, as does the income gained through postseason attendance. And Musial continued to lead the Cardinals to championships during the war years after Rickey was replaced at that position by William Walsingham, who had completed his unlikely rise from ticket taker in the organization. That St. Louis remains one of three teams in major league history to win at least one hundred games in three consecutive seasons after having achieved that feat during the war years upon the arrival of Musial is no coincidence.

Stan the Man established his greatness in 1943 by leading the league in batting average (.357), hits (220), doubles (48), triples (20), on-base percentage (.425), and slugging percentage (.562), and in earning his first Most Valuable Player award. Those who claimed the loss of pitching talent in the National League to the war effort cheapened his accomplishment had nothing to say after Musial returned from his own duty overseas in 1946 to pace the NL in all the same statistical categories aside from OBP to earn MVP honors again.

The following season proved tumultuous for Musial but allowed him to display both his morality and toughness. While some of his teammates protested vehemently against Jackie Robinson and his integration of major league baseball, Musial supported the rising Brooklyn star. Musial had championed African American teammates in high school and felt the need to do the same with Robinson, who later singled out the St. Louis legend for his appreciation.

Musial had his own problems in 1947. His .146 batting average through April required an explanation beyond a troubling slump, so he scheduled an exam with local physician and surgeon Robert Hyland, who diagnosed appendicitis and tonsilitis. Surgery for the former could have knocked Musial out for months, so Hyland performed a freezing operation on the appendix to shorten his absence to less than a week. Musial continued to struggle—his average remained under .200 into mid-June. He finally broke loose with a four-hit game against Brooklyn in late July and finished the season at .312.

The comparatively poor year proved to be an anomaly. What was not an anomaly was his team's absence from the World Series. The Cardinals had won pennants in four of his first five seasons but would not win another until 1964, the year after he retired. Musial performed beneath his standards in those events, batting just .256 with one home run and eight RBI in eighty-six at-bats. He managed just one hit in fourteen at-bats in games that clinched the series.

Such unproductiveness when it counted most never negatively affected the workmanlike Musial the following year. And when the Cardinals plunged into a rare period of mediocrity in the 1950s, his brilliance prevented them from far worse fates. The most glaring example was in 1955, when St. Louis stumbled to its worst record since 1924 as the offense around him collapsed. Musial carried the Redbirds that season—

his combined RBI and runs scored represented nearly one-third of the team total. Only the blossoming of third baseman Ken Boyer kept Stan the Man from being the only man who could produce for the Cardinals the following year.

Despite his quiet confidence, Musial shared moments of bravado. In 1955, during one of his twenty-four All-Star Game appearances (tied with Willie Mays and Hank Aaron for the most through 2021), he stepped into the batter's box against Red Sox right-hander Frank Sullivan and made a bold prediction after catcher Yogi Berra complained that his feet were killing him. "Relax, I'll have you home in a minute," Musial proclaimed. He then homered on the next pitch, one of an MLB-record six in his career.[7]

And when many assumed he was on the doorstep of fading away after batting .255 at age thirty-eight in 1959, he rebounded to finish with a flourish. Musial rededicated himself to conditioning after that season and even accepted a $20,000 pay cut from his $100,000 salary. Though he never again reached five hundred at-bats in a season, his performance improved over each of the next three. Musial even achieved a renaissance in 1962 at the age of forty-one, batting .330 with nineteen home runs and eighty-three RBI in just 135 games to place tenth in MVP balloting.

He announced his retirement in 1963 but remained a fixture with the Cardinals after owner Gussie Busch placed him into a front office position. Musial was promoted to general manager in 1967 and earned the distinction of becoming the only GM in baseball history to win a World Series in his only year on the job.

He had other fish to fry in his professional and personal life. Musial not only became involved in the real estate business but also opened a restaurant along with friend Julius "Biggie" Garangani called Stan and Biggie's. Garangani had piqued Musial's interest in politics in the late 1950s. Musial became active in the John F. Kennedy campaign for president in 1960 after having supported Republican Dwight Eisenhower during his presidency. A grateful Kennedy even presented Musial with a pin at a formal ceremony, prompting the latter to refer to the former as "my buddy." Fellow Democrat Lyndon Johnson, who assumed office after Kennedy was murdered, hired Musial as his physical fitness advisor.

Musial, who was inducted into the Hall of Fame in 1969, remained active in the restaurant business and other endeavors despite advancing age. He took care of beloved wheelchair-bound wife, Lillian, who suffered from heart problems and arthritis. Musial died on January 19, 2013, just eight months after Lillian passed away. President Barack Obama, who had two years earlier awarded him with the prestigious Presidential Medal of Freedom, spoke of his legacy upon his passing, saying, "Stan remains, to this day, an icon, untarnished; a beloved pillar of the community, a gentleman you'd want your kids to emulate."[8]

He indeed had become legend, not merely for his epic achievements on the diamond, but also for the humbleness, dignity, and good nature he displayed in all aspects of his life.

CHAPTER ELEVEN

From Contender to Pretender

THE TORCH WAS PASSED IN THE LATE 1940S AND REMAINED OUT OF THE hands of the Cardinals for nearly two decades. A new era in the National League had begun, not so coincidentally, after Robinson integrated the sport by joining Brooklyn. The Dodgers and crosstown New York Giants became kingpins of the senior circuit, winning eight of the next ten pennants, including every one from 1951 to 1956.

Not that St. Louis foundered that entire time. The club remained strong for several seasons after snagging the World Series crown in 1946. But it lacked hitting depth beyond Musial, Slaughter, and future manager Red Schoendienst. The Cardinals also struggled to find consistently strong starting pitching. Hurlers such as Gerry Staley and Harvey Haddix burst upon the scene but failed to maintain their effectiveness for more than a few years.

The result was winning records but mostly non-contention. One exception was 1949, when despite a distinct lack of power, the Cardinals rode a productive offense and a second twenty-win season from southpaw Howie Pollet into a fierce battle for the NL championship. They led the pack—barely—through most of late July into late September. But they stunningly dropped four straight on the road to lowly Pittsburgh and Chicago to blow a World Series berth.

Manager Eddie Dyer was not long for the job. He resigned after the Cardinals barely exceeded .500 in 1950 and was replaced the next season by scrappy shortstop Marty Marion, who had been forced due to a torn cartilage suffered the previous year to retire as a player. Principal owner

Fred Saigh believed the highly intelligent Marion would quickly earn the respect of his players despite his lack of experience as a manager. But his relationship with Saigh quickly turned sour after the injury-plagued Cardinals fell out of the race by mid-June and required a hot September to win eighty-one games. Marion often skipped town to be with his family and attend to business interests rather than stick around to discuss with Saigh about how to improve the team. Saigh wasted no time after that year canning Marion, who took over the same job with the miserable St. Louis Browns in 1952.

Saigh soon chose another hardnosed shortstop to assume the managerial position. And that was Eddie Stanky, who had established himself as one of the premier leadoff hitters in the game during his career with the Dodgers and Giants. Nicknamed "The Brat" for his combative style on the field and personality, Stanky, who served as player-manager but mostly kept himself on the bench, tolerated nothing less than passionate performance from his players. He fined those who failed to advance runners as he did so adeptly, confronted players who did not embrace a highly aggressive style of play, and developed adversarial relationships with the media. "He wanted you to play as if today's game was our first and last," said shortstop Dick Schofield.[1]

That attitude worked for a while. Stanky used the lefty-righty bullpen duo of Al Brazle and Eddie Uhas expertly in relief of mediocre starters to win one close game after another. He refused to allow his players to hoist the white flag after falling 13.5 games behind in late July despite completing a ten-game winning streak earlier that month. His team could not seriously threaten the eventual champion Dodgers but did sneak to within 6.5 games of the lead in early September. Their persistence earned Stanky National League Manager of the Year honors.

But what was accepted as spunky toughness when the Cardinals won was rejected by the players as abrasiveness when they lost. He failed to understand that not every inning of a 162-game schedule can be played by every player with maximum intensity. St. Louis decreased its win total every year under Stanky.

New owner Gussie Busch fired general manager William Washington in 1953 and replaced him with the wholly inexperienced Richard

Meyer, whose claim to fame had been working as an executive under him at the brewery. The stability that had played a significant role in the success of the franchise over the years was soon shaken. Meyer was fired two years later in favor of the infamous Frank "Trader" Lane, who finally gave way to Bing Devine in 1957. The last hire placed the club back on solid ground.

By that time the Cardinals had suffered through three consecutive losing seasons for the first time since 1918–1920. But the struggling team did introduce fine young hitting talent, including back-to-back Rookie of the Year winners Wally Moon and Bill Virdon, as well as Boyer, whose career achievements eventually overshadowed those of both and eventually won National League Most Valuable Player honors in the World Series championship season of 1964.

Another significant development during the down years was the breaking of the color line in 1954 by first baseman Tom Alston and pitcher Brooks Lawrence seven years after Robinson first integrated major league baseball. Alston failed to blossom, and Lawrence struggled after a sizzling start, but the Cardinals eventually emerged as a hotbed of tremendous black talent in the late 1950s and beyond when they added stars such as Curt Flood, Bill White, Lou Brock, and Bob Gibson.

Lane did the organization no favors during his short tenure before moving on to Cleveland, where he became one of the most ignominious figures in the history of that franchise when he traded revered slugger Rocky Colavito to Detroit for singles hitter Harvey Kuenn in the mistaken notion that power was overrated. Lane made what even he described as the worst trade in his career when he swapped Virdon, who was coming off his Rookie of the Year season, for good-field, no-hit center fielder Bobby DelGreco, DelGreco batted a miserable .215 for St. Louis in 1956 before continuing his destiny as a journeyman while Virdon served ten years as a dependable outfielder for Pittsburgh.

Potentially far more damaging from a public-relations standpoint was Lane's attempt to deal Stan Musial to Philadelphia for eventual Hall of Fame pitcher Robin Roberts. Though Musial had reached his mid-thirties, he remained an annual MVP candidate and even won a batting title in 1957. The younger Roberts was a six-time twenty-game

Steady and productive Bill White played on two World Series championship teams in the 1960s.
PHOTO COURTESY OF THE BASEBALL HALL OF FAME AND MUSEUM

winner but would after the trade speculation slip into mediocrity. Busch would have none of it. He stepped in to halt the proceedings in the justified fear of how fans would react to the loss of Musial.

The Lane era indeed proved tumultuous. It also highlighted Busch's inexperience as a baseball team owner. In his search for a general manager, he took the recommendation of *Sporting News* publisher J.G. Taylor to make his choice. Lane had established his reputation as a mad swapper in seven years with the White Sox, completing a ridiculous 241 trades, but that club had improved during his tenure. Spink offered in a column that "probably the most exciting chapter in the history of St. Louis baseball is about to be enacted . . . the Cardinals will have a team that will win more games . . . or the players who lose won't be around long."[2]

Lane wasted no time deceiving Busch and the fans. He claimed he would never trade Musial, Red Schoendienst, Moon, Boyer, Harvey Haddix, and a few other Cardinal players. He eventually sent several of them packing. He not only swapped Virdon for Del Greco, but he moved Schoendienst to the Giants for Alvin Dark in a deal featuring aging infielders. In a far worse trade, he sent Haddix, who remained a viable and consistent starting pitcher, and struggling reliever but eventual all-star Stu Miller, to the Giants for all-but-cooked starters Murry Dickson and Herm Wehmeier.

Busch became alarmed at rumored trades of St. Louis stars, including Musial and the beloved, blossoming Boyer, whom Lane reportedly sought to swap for Phillies standout hitter Richie Ashburn in another example of the GM's misguided belief that home runs were overvalued—the Philadelphia outfielder slugged a mere twenty-nine over the fence during his fifteen-year career. Lane had certainly not improved the club, which continued to lose. "If the Cardinals don't win this year or next, Frank Lane will be out on his ass," Busch promised a Knights of Columbus audience before the 1957 season.[3]

The proclamation irked Lane, who failed to negotiate an extended contract even after Del Ennis, his veteran trade acquisition from Philadelphia, drove in 102 runs to help the Cardinals win eighty-seven games. Lane resigned after that season with one year remaining on his contract. Busch soon replaced him with Devine, whose moves helped transform the team into a two-time World Series champion.

By that time, the franchise had also experienced an overhaul at the managerial position. Stanky was fired thirty-six games into the 1955 season by Busch, who, in the words of *Time* magazine, believed "The Brat" was (in appropriate beer-baron terms) "too much foam and not enough body."[4] He was replaced by Harry "The Hat" Walker, who lost his job soon thereafter (and would not land another manager job for ten years) when Lane sent him packing in favor of former Tigers skipper Fred Hutchinson.

The Hutchinson-Lane combination was not made in baseball heaven. The two squabbled about strategy. One notable clash occurred in July 1957, after Hutchinson left southpaw Wilmer "Vinegar Bend"

Mizell in to pitch against Dodgers slugger Gil Hodges, who smashed a grand slam to turn a 9–5 Cardinals lead into a tie and eventual defeat that pushed them out of first place. During a closed-door meeting after learning that Lane vehemently and publicly questioned not replacing Mizell, Hutchinson lashed out. "I've got to be left alone to do my job," he fumed. "It's hard enough to fight the opposition on the field every day without answering to my own front office in the newspapers. Criticize me all you want. Second-guess me in private. I get paid to take that. But when your criticism hits every newspaper in the country, it can wreck the morale of this ballclub. That's one thing we can't stand."[5]

The animosity that permeated through the top of the organization might have cost St. Louis the 1957 pennant. The club won fifteen of nineteen following the rift but was eventually worn down. A nine-game losing streak that included six defeats to the terrible Cubs and three to the first-place Braves—the team they were chasing—all but destroyed their season. They rebounded to pull to within 2.5 games of the top but could not overcome the drought.

Hutchinson did not endear himself to Busch either, particularly in 1958 over a disagreement about the merits of Tom Alston, the first black player in franchise history. The owner wanted Alston in the lineup, but the manager did not believe Alston was the second coming of Lou Gehrig. Hutchinson, in fact, compared Alston to a legendary clown: "Mr. Busch, do you want me to say what I really think or what you want to hear?" he asked. "If I wanted to play a clown, I'd go hire Emmett Kelly."[6]

The relationship between the owner, GM, and manager was untenable. And it didn't last long. Lane and Hutchinson were both gone by the end of the 1958 season. Mediocrity continued for a few years thereafter. But Devine was building something quite divine.

CHAPTER TWELVE

Steal of a Swap and a Harrowing Race

THE NOTION THAT THE ARRIVAL OF BING DEVINE AS GENERAL MANager magically transformed the Cardinals into winners is false. That his hiring planted the seeds for success is certainly true. The club simply needed to dump a wildly unpopular manager to achieve its goals.

That skipper was Solly Hemus, who was still an active player when Busch brought him in to replace Fred Hutchinson. Hemus had, in fact, played three strong seasons in St. Louis early that decade before losing playing time and serving as a reserve with Philadelphia. He had yearned to manage and toward that end sent a fawning letter to Busch following his trade to the Phillies praising him for the job he had done as owner of the Cardinals and expressing a desire to eventually return in some capacity.

Little could the thirty-five-year-old Hemus have imagined that opportunity would arrive as big-league manager in 1959. And little could he have imagined that it would all go so terribly wrong so fast. He lost his first three games that season and panicked, altering lineups and even moving slumping superstar Stan Musial down to sixth in the batting order from the third spot in which he had thrived for years. St. Louis plummeted into the cellar and remained there until mid-May. The team recovered to sneak over .500 but lost twenty-five of thirty-four late in the year to drop into seventh place in an eight-team league. By that time, he was among the most despised managers in franchise history, criticizing players in front of his teammates about play on the field and continuing his condemnations well after games were over.

"Solly was easily despised," said pitcher Jim Brosnan, whose baseball career was followed by success as an author. "I thought he could have been a very good manager because of his knowledge, but he simply did not know how to handle different types of people."[1]

The Cardinals certainly had become far more diverse and talented by 1959. Devine had done his best to improve the roster. Before Hemus even donned a St. Louis uniform, the GM had stolen first baseman Bill White from the Giants for three inexperienced pitchers. White, who had lost his job in San Francisco to future Hall of Famer Orlando Cepeda after returning from two years of military service, blossomed into a consistent slugger and perennial all-star. Devine had earlier in the offseason apparently worn a mask in robbing Cincinnati of talented nineteen-year-old outfielder Curt Flood. Meanwhile, promising right-hander Bob Gibson had rocketed through the minor league system and was about to make his debut.

The three future black stars could have enjoyed smooth sailing in their early years with St. Louis if Busch had not insisted that Devine hire Hemus as manager. Flood became the first victim when he was benched and used mostly as a defensive replacement after starting slowly at the plate in 1959. Hemus's racial insensitivity proved most damaging to his relationships with his black players. His feelings became quite clear to them when he called Pittsburgh pitcher Bennie Daniels a "black bastard" after sticking out his leg and taking an intentional hit-by-pitch during one of his infrequent playing appearances that year.

"Until then, we detested Hemus for not using the best lineup," Flood wrote in his autobiography. "Now we hated him for himself." Offered Gibson: "Either he disliked us deeply or he genuinely believed that the way to motivate us was with insults." So infuriated and fed up had Gibson become with Hemus that he decided to quit the team. Only the reassuring words of coach Harry Walker prevented Gibson from leaving the club. "He'll be gone long before you will," Walker told him.[2]

Walker was right. But Hemus lasted longer than many expected, greatly because the forgiving Musial told Busch that the manager should be given another chance to prove himself. And despite the fact that Hemus even benched the legendary Musial at times early in 1960

Curt Flood botched a fly ball in Game 7 in 1968 but otherwise performed well in St. Louis before taking a stand against the reserve clause.

PHOTO COURTESY OF THE BASEBALL HALL OF FAME AND MUSEUM

and only returned him to the lineup due to injuries while Flood and Gibson still struggled, the Cardinals did rebound in the second half to finish 86–68. Hemus patched together a vastly improved pitching staff with just two full-time starters in Larry Jackson, who led the league in innings pitched, and Ray Sadecki. He even coaxed twenty-one wins out of young Ernie Broglio, who started twenty-four games and relieved in twenty-eight more while Lindy McDaniel emerged as a lights-out closer with twenty-seven saves. The Cardinals threw a scare into the eventual world champion Pirates, winning twice in Pittsburgh in mid-August to pull within three games of first place before faltering.

The turnaround did not soothe player feelings toward Hemus. It merely delayed the inevitable. The Cardinals began losing the close games in 1961 that they had won the season before. An 8–17 stretch early that year doomed the unpopular skipper, who received a pink slip on Independence Day. Devine could finally select the manager he wanted. He promoted coach and former minor league manager Johnny Keane to his first managerial job.

The Redbirds did not take flight from the start of the Keane era. They rebounded in 1961 to finish over .500 as Devine continued to reshape the roster under pressure from an increasingly impatient Busch. He had resurrected the career of aging left-hander Curt Simmons, who had appeared doomed by shoulder and elbow injuries that had sidelined him with the Phillies. He proved that gas remained in the tank upon his arrival in St. Louis and emerged as one of its premier starters during its pennant race run in 1963 and its capturing of the crown a year later. Devine also acquired veteran shortstop Dick Groat from Pittsburgh heading into the 1963 season. The 1960 NL Most Valuable Player played a critical role in helping the Cardinals take the title in 1964.

By that time, Busch had hired ancient Branch Rickey as a front office advisor who reported directly to the owner. Devine did not welcome the venerable former general manager. When asked by Rickey in late 1962, "Are we going to have any trouble if I'm here to run the club?" Devine replied, "We *have* trouble right now."[3]

Those were among the last words Rickey and Devine spoke to one another. Yet their relationship worked on a professional level, and Busch proved his independence from the former when he greenlighted the Groat trade despite Rickey's recommendation to the contrary.

Devine did not allow any friction with Rickey to negatively affect his job performance—he simply did not believe he needed the assistance. His track record spoke for itself. In 1959, he had apparently donned a mask to steal Broglio from San Francisco for three nonentities. Broglio became attractive enough to other clubs to be offered as a trade piece in one of the most lopsided deals in baseball history.

With premier hitters such as Flood, White, and Boyer in their prime and rookie catcher Tim McCarver contributing at a high level, the 1963 Cardinals led the National League in runs scored under Keane despite the understandable lack of production from the forty-three-year-old Musial in his final season. The mound triumvirate of Simmons, Broglio, and the emerging Gibson performed well enough to keep St. Louis in the pennant race throughout against the Dodgers, which featured one of the greatest pitching staffs in baseball history.

Such heady aspirations seemed unlikely to be fulfilled after the Cardinals were swept in Los Angeles in early July to set off a 4–10 stretch that pushed them seven games out. They remained the same distance behind in late August before embarking on an incredible run to the top. A 19–1 blitz that included two nine-game winning streaks placed them one game behind the Dodgers with a home series against that team next on the schedule. Rare weeknight crowds of thirty thousand poured into Busch Stadium to watch the showdowns, but they all left disappointed as Los Angeles completed a sweep. Otherworldly southpaw Sandy Koufax highlighted the set with a four-hit shutout in outbattling Simmons. The Redbirds were reeling—they lost six straight to fall out of contention. Soon their fans were relegated to rooting for Musial to go out with a bang and being satisfied with his last-at-bat single.

Yet despite the collapse, one could not be too disappointed. The club featured an ideal mix of talented youth and veterans. Devine remained driven to strengthen the team. And on June 15, 1964, he pulled arguably the greatest rip-off in the history of the sport. But little could anyone have predicted how lopsided the trade that brought left fielder Lou Brock to St. Louis in exchange for Broglio would be. In fact, some considered it to heavily favor the Cubs when it was engineered. Among them was *Chicago Daily News* sportswriter Bob Smith, who offered the following:

Thank you, thank you, oh, you lovely St. Louis Cardinals. Nice doing business with you. Please call again any time.[4]

The St. Louis media and fans were not exactly turning cartwheels. "They wanted to run [Devine] out of town at first," said Cardinals first baseman Mike Shannon. "But as players, we knew the possibility of Lou."[5]

So did Keane. He greeted Brock upon his arrival by accompanying him to left field at Busch Stadium. "It's a big [outfield], and it's all yours," Keane told him. "If you can do what I think you can, you ought to be able to play out here the rest of your life."[6]

Brock was terrified. He knew that Devine had unloaded one of the better pitchers in the National League. What nobody knew was that the injury-plagued Broglio would win just seven games the rest of his career. At the time, the pressure on Brock was enormous. "It was like being in a prison yard with everyone waiting for you to do something wrong," he said. "There was the thrill, yes, of coming to the major leagues—but I was scared to death."[7]

The ultimate success of the 1964 Cardinals did not coincide directly with the Brock acquisition. They had lost five straight, including two to the miserable Houston Colt 45s, when he first donned a St. Louis uniform on June 16. Their 28–31 record had plunged them into eighth place in what became a ten-team lead in 1962. After Keane placed Brock second in the lineup behind Flood, the newcomer began his arduous climb from .251 to a year-end average of .315. But the Redbirds did not get their wings off the ground with him immediately. They won four straight upon his arrival, then descended again while Brock embarked on a thirteen-game hitting streak.

They finally took off in late July. A 35–15 blitz into mid-September vaulted them into second place, but not before a feud between Groat and Devine cost the latter his job. The blowup was precipitated by Keane giving Groat the green light to call hit-and-run plays at the plate. But several failures motivated the manager to turn that light red. An angry

Hall of Fame speedster Lou Brock came from the Cubs in one of the most lopsided trades in major league history.
PHOTO COURTESY OF THE BASEBALL HALL OF FAME AND MUSEUM

Groat stopped talking to Keane, so Devine called a meeting so the two could hash out their differences. All appeared fine when Groat apologized to the team, but Busch fired Devine weeks later because he felt slighted over having been kept in the dark. The owner wondered if other personnel matters had been hidden from him.

Second or third place appeared to be the team's destiny. After all, the Phillies remained six games ahead with no sign of slowing down. Their lead shrank by just one game with eleven left to play. It was expected that the Cardinals would soon be playing for nothing but pride.

Then it happened—the most epic end-of-the-year collapse in baseball history. The Phillies stopped hitting. Then they stopped pitching. They lost seven straight at home to Cincinnati and Milwaukee. Their lead was gone when they arrived in St. Louis for a do-or-die series with five games remaining on their schedule.

The Cardinals owned all the momentum, and they flew with it. Gibson and new ace reliever Barney Schultz, whom Devine received from the Cubs nine days after the Brock trade, shut down Philadelphia in the opener. St. Louis left-hander Ray Sadecki earned his twentieth win with help from Schultz in the middle game of the series, then the Cardinals bashed the Phillies into oblivion with fourteen hits in an 8–5 victory.

The job was not done. Cincinnati had also snuck up from behind. The Reds had even forged ahead after winning nine straight. They lost four of five, but St. Louis dropped two to the pathetic Mets. It seemed no team wanted the pennant. The Reds and Cardinals began the last day of the season tied for the top. The former fell to Philadelphia, while the latter finally broke out their bats with eight extra-base hits, including homers by White and Flood, to destroy the Mets and capture the pennant. The Redbirds were headed to a showdown with the Yankees, which stunningly and unknowingly was about to compete in the last World Series of their four-decade dynasty.

It was a typical Fall Classic. The series featured memorable moments. Legendary Yankees slugger Mickey Mantle won Game 3 with a walk-off home run off Schultz. Young St. Louis right-hander Ron Taylor no-hit the Bronx Bombers over the last four innings in a taut Game 4 to tie the series. Gibson pitched ten scintillating innings with thirteen strikeouts to snag a Game 5 victory that was all but clinched by a three-run homer from battery mate Tim McCarver. Emerging New York starter Jim Bouton, who had gained notoriety in the previous World Series for throwing with such force that his cap flew off his head on nearly every pitch, performed brilliantly and benefited from a Joe Pepitone grand slam for a win two days later that forced a deciding game at Busch Stadium.

With Gibson mowing down the Yankees, it appeared his team was in for smooth sailing when it forged ahead 6–0 into the sixth. But pitching on just two days' rest, Gibson finally tired. Two singles and another Mantle blast chopped the lead to 6–3. Keane rode Gibson throughout. The right-hander worked fast so his opponents at the plate would not notice his fatigue. His teammates later admitted they heard Gibson grunt on every pitch from the seventh inning forward.

"Don't be cute, and don't go for the corners," Keane advised Gibson, heading into a ninth inning with their team ahead 9–5. "They're not going to hit four home runs off you."[8]

No, but they did hit two. Clete Boyer and Phil Linz took Gibson deep before Bobby Richardson, who had set a World Series record with thirteen hits, popped out to end it as the pitching hero was mobbed by teammates and fans who dropped over the outfield walls to join in the celebration. The Cardinals owned their first world championship in eighteen years—a veritable drought for arguably the most successful franchise in National League history.

Asked after the game why he never summoned a reliever, Keane gave a reply that spoke to his respect for Gibson as a pitcher and as a man. "He didn't pitch only with his arm," Keane said. "He pitched with his heart. He's got lots of heart . . . I went all the way with him because I was committed to his heart."[9]

What Keane was not committed to was the organization. Still angry over the firing of Devine in August and rumors of his own professional demise down the stretch of the regular season, he threw Busch a curve the day after the team clinched the crown. The Cardinals called a press conference to announce that Keane would indeed be back in 1965. Keane stunned Busch and new GM Bob Howsam, as well as the assembled media, by instead handing the owner a letter of resignation. The dramatic moment, which occurred on the same day the Yankees canned manager Yogi Berra, ended Keane's thirty-five-year affiliation with the franchise. The stunning events took an even wilder turn when Keane replaced Berra as New York manager in 1965, got fired a year later, and died unexpectedly in January 1967.

The 1964 Cardinals proved more than their claim as the best team in baseball. During an era of racial inequality and strife, they showed that blacks and whites could work together and even forge friendships to achieve a common goal. "The Cardinals were the rare team that not only believed in each other, but genuinely liked each other," wrote Gibson. "As a team, we would simply not tolerate any sort of festering rancor between us, personal or racial. We brought our racial feelings out into the open and dealt with them. . . . I'm confident I had a lot to do with it, and so did guys like White and Flood. . . . None of us gave an inch to racism. The white player respected that . . . and in turn we respected them. . . . Of all the teams I played on . . . there was never a better band of men than the '64 Cardinals."[10]

The Yankees dynasty ended under Keane, but the Cardinals thrived as the turbulent 1960s continued. And it was Gibson who led the way.

CHAPTER THIRTEEN

Bullet Bob

BASEBALL CAREERS ARE MOST OFTEN DEFINED BY ACHIEVEMENTS. THEY are examined and judged statistically. Bob Gibson would have been a first-ballot Hall of Famer based on numbers and accomplishments alone. There were the five twenty-win seasons in six years. There was the record-setting 1.12 earned run average in 1968. There were the brilliant World Series performances in 1964, 1967, and 1968.

But one cannot analyze Gibson by simply citing statistics and successes on the mound. His greatness was fueled not only by stuff. It reflected attitude, grit, fierce competitiveness, the way he stared down and intimidated batters. Nobody understood that better or admired it more than longtime battery mate Tim McCarver, who encapsulated the Gibson mystique in the following passage of his 1987 autobiography, titled *Oh Baby, I Love It*:

> *For my money, the most intimidating, arrogant pitcher ever to kick up dirt on the mound is Bob Gibson. . . . If you ever saw Gibson work, you'd never forget his style: his cap pulled down low over his eyes, the ball gripped—almost mashed—behind his right hip, the eyes smoldering at each batter almost accusingly. . . . (He) didn't like to lose to anyone in anything. . . . Bob was a man of mulish competitive instinct.*[1]

Unlike many of his African American brethren in major league baseball born and raised in areas of the country that mandated Jim Crow laws that stifled educational opportunities, Gibson lived in the far

Catcher Tim McCarver played his first eleven seasons with St. Louis and nearly captured NL MVP honors in 1967.

PHOTO COURTESY OF THE BASEBALL HALL OF FAME AND MUSEUM

Bob Gibson was not only one of the premier pitchers in baseball history, but perhaps the gutsiest in World Series competition.
PHOTO COURTESY OF THE BASEBALL HALL OF FAME AND MUSEUM

less suffocating city of Omaha, Nebraska. He was born on November 9, 1935, as the youngest of seven children. Not that the family thrived financially—his father died of tuberculosis before he was born, and his mother, Victoria, toiled at a laundromat and by cleaning homes to feed, clothe, and house her children.

Among those kids was eldest son and surrogate father, Josh, whose positive influence on Bob allowed him to pursue his dreams. Josh passed on a value of education, particularly after he received a degree in history from Creighton University. He proved to be an ideal role model for his youngest brother. Josh worked as a recreation director near their Omaha home, mentoring boys such as Bob who lived in the projects.

"Josh led by example," Gibson recalled. "He required no more from any of us than he gave himself. . . . He would have loved to have the opportunity . . . to pursue a career in professional sports. . . . But since that avenue was closed for him—the color barriers were not broken in time to help Josh—he did as he told me I would otherwise have to do: He got an education. . . . We were all, one way or another, a reflection of Josh."[2]

Major health problems in his youth seemed to preclude the possibility that Bob would blossom into a professional athlete at any level. He suffered from rickets, pneumonia, asthma, hay fever, and a heart issue. But he was driven to succeed. Gibson eventually joined the baseball and basketball teams Josh organized. The younger sibling displayed versatility both in the field as a catcher, shortstop, and pitcher and as a switch-hitter who made consistent hard contact and showed power potential. At age fifteen, he helped the Y Monarchs become the first black team in Omaha to win the American Legion crown and earned all-city honors.

The ugly specter of racism soon pushed a roadblock into Gibson's budding baseball career. He was barred from playing that sport as a junior at Omaha Technical High School supposedly for reporting a day late for tryouts, but in reality, as Gibson would discover to his dismay years later, because the coach did not allow black players. That merely strengthened his desire to seek a career in basketball, which he embraced as his favorite sport anyway. It also allowed him to thrive in track. Gibson set an Omaha high school record in the high jump. His future sport became further muddled when he was a senior, when a new coach who allowed him to compete stuck him in the lineup and watched him bat .368, which ranked second in the city.

Some believed his most promising sport was basketball—he accepted a scholarship to play hoops at Creighton University after the University of Indiana shunned him because it had already reached its quota of black athletes. Gibson was torn between basketball and baseball, in which he also competed at Creighton. He even hooked up with the legendary Harlem Globetrotters for one winter. The deadly serious and intense Gibson did not fit in with the fun-loving group, but his expectation of always winning certainly did.

Circumstances made the decision for Gibson. He simply faced a greater opportunity on the diamond than on the hardcourt. He led the Nebraska College Conference with a .333 batting average and again proved his versatility by winning six of eight decisions on the mound. Though no major league club, including St. Louis, made overwhelming offers, he received nary a word from any NBA club aside from the Minneapolis Lakers. And that team, which had sunk to the bottom of the league by that time after a period of domination, never sought to sign Gibson. Baseball was his future by default.

The Cardinals showed optimism about his future by immediately placing him at Triple-A Omaha, where Gibson would not only be one step from the big leagues but pitching in his hometown. He also enjoyed the good fortune of playing for manager Johnny Keane, who treated all his charges well regardless of skin color. "[Keane] had no prejudices concerning my color," Gibson said. "He was the closest thing to a saint that I ever came across in baseball."[3]

Too bad race relations weren't saintlier in the South when Gibson, who struggled particularly with his control during his first stint in Omaha, was sent to Class A Columbus (Georgia) to compete in the South Atlantic League. Bigotry proved more daunting than the competition on the field. He had been keenly aware of racism growing up in Omaha but not about the stifling institutionalized discrimination of his new environment until experiencing it personally. Segregation remained all-encompassing in Columbus in the late 1950s, as well as in the other cities he visited. He was forced to live and eat apart from his white teammates. He was taunted unmercifully by Southern fans still clinging to the "glories" of the Confederacy. The mound proved to be his only sanctuary, but he again struggled to find the strike zone consistently.

The lone encouragement was that the Cardinals needed pitching. He performed better with their Triple-A clubs in Omaha and Rochester in 1958, earning kudos from managers as owning the best fastball in the league and improving his control dramatically, though it would not be until 1962 that the pinpoint accuracy that would become legend became pronounced. He had earned candidacy for the St. Louis rotation heading into the 1959 season.

There was one huge problem—his name was Solly Hemus. Gibson felt the negative racial views of the new Cardinals manager had temporarily wrecked his confidence. The twenty-three-year-old had yet to establish his mental and emotional toughness, and he allowed Hemus to bring him down. Gibson earned a roster spot out of the bullpen and was quickly demoted after three appearances. "Hemus had me convinced that I wasn't any damn good and, consequently, I wasn't," he wrote in his autobiography. Gibson finally arrived to stay in June 1960 and somehow felt a small sense of optimism that Hemus would come around. "My best hope lay in the fact that Hemus, as much as he seemed to dislike me, might not really *know* me," he added in his book. "He kept calling me Bridges, confusing me with Marshall Bridges, who was several years old than me, skinnier, and pitched left-handed. But he was black. Solly got *that* much right."[4]

Teammate Curt Flood complained that Hemus used Gibson only when no other pitcher was available. Gibson's crisis of confidence continued in 1960 as his control worsened, resulting in a 5.63 ERA and a spot in the back of the bullpen. But even Hemus could not keep Gibson down the following year. By the time Hemus was mercifully fired and replaced by the beloved Keane, he had planted the seeds of his greatness. He had earned four complete-game victories in one month, including a shutout of the Cubs during which he struck out eleven. Though he performed sporadically the rest of that season, he felt far more at ease with Keane at the helm and established himself as a rotation mainstay by winning five of his last seven decisions.

The rest of Gibson's career—at least until he approached forty—was defined by consistent brilliance, his win totals more a reflection of a lack of run support than performance. With his intimidating mound presence, including the steely stares at batters, his intensity played as strong a role in his success as his stuff. But his pure talent translated into all-star appearances and Cy Young Awards once he learned to control his fastball and slider. He recorded significantly fewer walks in more innings in 1962 than he had the previous year and was on his way.

Attitude and ability combined to make Gibson one of the most consistently dominant pitchers of his era. He posted a winning record every year from 1961 to 1973. Over the last eight seasons in that incredible run, during which he won at least twenty-five times, he managed an ERA of 3.12 or lower. The lowered mound in 1969 designed to encourage more offense in a stiflingly boring game affected him little. He managed a 2.18 ERA that year.

In the midst of all that consistency and success, Gibson did rise to a nearly unthinkable level in 1968, which became forever known as the Year of the Pitcher, greatly because of his mind-boggling performance. Gibson set a major league record that still stood through 2021 and perhaps forever by posting a 1.12 ERA. He hurled a remarkable thirteen shutouts along the way, including three that extended into an extra inning. Gibson allowed more than three earned runs just once in a nine-inning game all year. That he earned both Cy Young and NL Most Valuable Player honors proved as shocking as the sun rising in the east. "He carried the whole team," remarked teammate and 1967 MVP Orlando Cepeda. "He should get all the awards that are presented."[5]

By that time, admiration for Gibson had been established by his peers that extended far beyond his pitching talents. Even supreme slugger Hank Aaron, who could not be intimidated easily, admitted his fear of the St. Louis superstar to young teammate Dusty Baker. "Don't dig in against Bob Gibson, he'll knock you down," Aaron said. "He'd knock down his own grandmother if she dared to challenge him. Don't stare at him, don't smile at him, don't talk to him. He doesn't like it. If you happen to hit a home run, don't run too slow, don't run too fast. If you happen to want to celebrate, get in the tunnel first. And if he hits you, don't charge

After arriving from San Francisco, Orlando Cepeda earned his only MVP award with St. Louis to help the team to a world title.

PHOTO COURTESY OF THE BASEBALL HALL OF FAME AND MUSEUM

the mound because he's a Gold Glove boxer. I'm like, damn, what about my seventeen-game hitting streak? That was the night it ended."[6]

It can hardly be imagined that the fierce competitiveness Gibson displayed during the regular season had another level. But it indeed reached one rarely seen in major league baseball with the Cardinals depending on him in the 1967 and 1968 World Series. He had already proven his guts and ability to rise to the occasion in the 1964 Fall Classic by hurling a complete-game victory on two days' rest to clinch the crown. But he had matured greatly three years later as a pitcher. That combination of athletic greatness and intensity proved deadly to the Red Sox and Tigers.

Though the Cardinals by that time boasted several premier starting pitchers, manager Red Schoendienst never hesitated to proclaim his ace by plotting Gibson for three starts in any seven-game series. That decision twice paid dividends despite the defeat in 1968. He proved more dominant in Series competition than during the regular season despite the stronger offensive talent. He fanned ninety-two batters in eighty-one innings against the Yankees, Red Sox, and Tigers combined.

Far more importantly, Gibson performed brilliantly in every Series start, particularly in 1967 and 1968. He carried the Cardinals to the title in 1967 with three of their four victories to subdue Boston, which had gathered momentum by winning the tightest pennant race in baseball history to complete its Impossible Dream season. Gibson finished his mastery of the Sox with a 1.00 ERA after having hurled a shutout in Game 4 and polished them off in the clincher with a complete-game, ten-strikeouts performance during which he even provided a home run off American League Cy Young Award–winner Jim Lonborg.

After setting the all-time single-season ERA record in 1968, Bullet Bob opened against Detroit with one of the greatest pitching efforts in baseball history. He established a new World Series record with seventeen strikeouts in thoroughly outperforming thirty-one-game winner Denny McLain for a 4–0 shutout. The Tigers marveled at the stuff they had yet to witness in the pre-interleague era. They expected Gibson to throw mostly fastballs, but he crossed them up by mixing in about 40 percent breaking balls. McLain, who bragged before the game that he wanted to "humiliate" and "demolish" the Cardinals, exclaimed that he had just witnessed "the greatest pitching performance I've seen in my life." When asked to capsulize his team's defeat, Detroit manager Mayo Smith similarly stated, "Gibson's a hell of a pitcher—that's the story of this game."[7]

He was merely warming up. Only a Jim Northrup home run in Game 4 prevented Gibson from pitching a second consecutive shutout. It appeared Gibson had put the Tigers away, but they clawed back to force a Game 7. He battled portly Detroit left-hander Mickey Lolich, who had usurped the role of ace from McLain in the series. Gibson remained on top of his game. He retired the first ten batters and maintained a one-hit shutout through 6.2 innings in a taut 0–0 game. Successive singles in the seventh brought Northrup to the plate. He hit a fly ball to center field that the usually reliable Flood misjudged. Flood sprinted in, tripped, and allowed it soar over his head to the wall. The two-run triple doomed St. Louis to defeat.

Age often lessens the effectiveness of pitchers, particularly those who lose velocity off their fastballs and must alter their approaches on the mound. Gibson was not among them. He remained one of the premier pitchers in the sport, throwing more breaking balls and winning a second Cy Young Award in 1970 after compiling a 23–7 record. He pitched even better in his late thirties than he had a decade earlier. He posted a tremendous 1.108 WHIP (walks and hits to innings pitched) at the age of thirty-seven in 1973. As usual, Gibson also helped himself that year, winning his ninth straight Gold Glove. That Gibson earned a reputation as one of the top fielding pitchers in major league history should surprise nobody. He never allowed self-deficiency in any area of his game. He retired after finally losing his stuff and sporting a 3–10 record in 1975.

Gibson still had much to offer the sport. He toiled as a broadcaster on the *ABC Monday Night Baseball* broadcasts and provided basketball commentary on the radio in New York and Atlanta. He hosted a Cardinals pregame show for KMOX-AM in the mid-1980s before landing a job with the ESPN baseball broadcast team in 1990.

A well-rounded perspective on life motivated Gibson to seek relevance in work beyond sports. Though he accepted several coaching jobs with the Cardinals and other major league teams, he delved into several commercial ventures in his hometown of Omaha, including a banking endeavor driven to help the African American community. His keen awareness of racism and anger heightened when he realized that many businesses declined to work with his black-owned company. Gibson also opened a restaurant near the Creighton University campus.

Not that all evolved swimmingly between Gibson and the Cardinals. He offered in his autobiography, entitled *Stranger to the Game*, that his views on issues such as race and his willingness to express them motivated the organization to blackball him from the game. He speculated that his 1981 Hall of Fame acceptance speech in which he failed unintentionally to credit ownership and management for their contributions to his career rankled franchise bigwigs despite the efforts of Gibson to apologize directly to Gussie Busch for the oversight. In summation, he wrote, "It baffles me . . . that baseball would feel so antagonistic toward me as to keep me out of its ranks when all I ever did was try to play it to the best of my ability."[8]

He also gave back to the sport in retirement as a member of the board of directors of the Baseball Assistance Team, which was formed to help players and their families deal with addictions and other psychological and emotional issues. But when he died in October 2020 after losing his battle with pancreatic cancer, it was all the winning battles with championships on the line and his fierce competitiveness that baseball fans would cherish the most in their memories.

Chapter Fourteen

Disappointment and Dominance

The Cardinals appeared destined to dominate in 1965 as defending World Series champions. Though they lacked pitching depth, the return of rotation stalwarts Bob Gibson, Curt Simmons, and Ray Sadecki seemed certain to repeat or at least approach their effectiveness in the previous season. And the young lineup featuring speedsters Lou Brock and Curt Flood as table setters for sluggers Ken Boyer and Bill White returned to frustrate opposing pitchers.

St. Louis fans were in for a letdown. Several of those standouts either performed well but not at the level reached in 1964, or they failed miserably. Brock batted .288 and launched in earnest his personal assault on the all-time career record in stolen bases (eventually broken by Rickey Henderson) by swiping sixty-three. Flood also repeated his brilliance from the season past, but neither White nor the aging Boyer produced to similar levels.

Offense, however, was not the primary problem. Instead, it was the deterioration of the Big Three down to the Big One—Gibson. Only Bullet Bob performed well on the mound. Age had finally caught up with the thirty-six-year-old Simmons, whose victory total was cut in half from eighteen to nine and whose ERA skyrocketed to 4.08 as his career began its fade.

But most pronounced and stunning among the disappointments was Sadecki, a twenty-game winner in 1964. The hard-throwing southpaw raised his strikeout rate in 1965 while all other aspects of his performance plummeted. He finished the season with a 6–15 record and a shocking

5.21 ERA. And that represented an improvement after a brutal first half. Sadecki got knocked out in the first inning twice in his first four starts, rebounded to pitch better in May, then lost his spot in the rotation after an awful four-start period during which he allowed sixteen runs in twelve innings. Soon his ERA ballooned to 7.11. By May 1966 he had been traded to San Francisco in a steal of a deal for super slugger Orlando Cepeda, who won NL Most Valuable Player honors for the Cardinals the following year.

Rather than criticize himself for performing poorly in 1965, Sadecki told others that he had overachieved the season before when they brought up his twenty wins. "I won ballgames that year where they pinch-hit for me the fifth, and they'd get the hit that puts you ahead, and then the bullpen holds them."[1]

That bullpen was anchored by Barney Schultz, who was among the many Cardinals who struggled in 1965. And though Hal Woodeshick (whose cousin Tom was a standout running back for the Philadelphia Eagles) replaced him effectively as the closer, the relief corps also took a step back.

The result of all the downturns in performance was felt immediately. The Redbirds lost five of their first six games and never fully recovered. They did win eleven of twelve in May to pull within 1.5 games of the top and even took two of three against the first-place Dodgers in Los Angeles. But a stretch that heading into the season would have seem unfathomable followed. The Cardinals lost sixteen of twenty-two in June to fall permanently out of the race and stumbled to finish under .500.

What seemed like an anomaly became alarming in 1966. And this time it was the hitting that deserved the blame. The offense descended from one of the best in baseball to the worst in the National League. They scored 136 fewer runs than they had the previous season despite leading the circuit in stolen bases and a strong year from Cepeda, Brock, and Shannon. The club simply could not overcome holes in the lineup, especially among infielders Dal Maxvill, Julian Javier, and Charley Smith. The Cardinals had sunk to ninth place by late May, and despite recovering to win eighty-three games, they never sniffed contention.

What they did sniff was the fresh grass in their brand-new home when they moved from what was originally called Sportsman's Park to

Busch Stadium on May 12. The former had hosted its last game four days earlier on the same grounds that had been used for baseball for one hundred years. That finale featured pomp and circumstance, such as pregame ceremonies honoring all-time great and one-year GM Stan Musial. The Giants ensured that the 17.503 patrons would return home unhappy by burying St. Louis, 10–5. But for Musial, the game was more about saying good-bye to an old friend of a ballpark. "They say diamonds are a girl's best friend, but this old diamond has been pretty good to us, Red," Musial told Red Schoendienst. The manager simply nodded.[2]

Far more St. Louis fans chose to attend the unveiling of the new ballpark. A parade preceded the game against Atlanta, which lured a crowd of 46,048. Veteran groundskeeper Bill Stocksick had added a bit of ceremonial flair to the proceedings, digging up home plate at the old venue and flying it via helicopter to the new one. And this time the Cardinals came through, beating the Braves in extra innings on a walk-off single by Brock.

Oddly, Cepeda played in both games—the first with San Francisco and the second with St. Louis. The lopsided swap that sent him to the Cardinals was announced shortly after the swan song at Sportsman's Park. But though Cepeda continued to hit for a high average after his arrival in 1966, the weakening home run and RBI numbers that motivated the Giants to trade him remained a problem.

The power shortage proved quite temporary. Cepeda keyed an offensive resurgence as the Cardinals finally provided Brock and Flood with protection. Cepeda led the team in doubles, home runs, RBI, on-base percentages, and slugging percentages in snagging NL MVP honors. He received plenty of help in the middle of the lineup from Shannon, McCarver, and even newcomer Roger Maris, who managed one last hurrah six years after breaking Babe Ruth's single-season home run record.

Yet one could argue that a twenty-two-year-old pitcher played as significant a role in the team's revival as Cepeda. And that was lanky left-hander Steve Carlton, who had received a taste of the big leagues the previous two seasons before landing a spot in the rotation in early May and running with it. Carlton performed brilliantly into early June, faltered for a month, then established himself as a steady and stingy starter the rest of the season, particularly down the stretch as the team pulled away from the pack and coasted to the crown.

Carlton was not the only hurler to rival Gibson as the staff ace—at least in the regular season. Bespectacled right-hander Dick Hughes, a quintessential flash-in-the-pan, came out of nowhere to post a 16–6 record and lead the rotation with a 2.67 ERA. He served in long relief early that year until a line drive off the bat of Pittsburgh super slugger Roberto Clemente nailed and knocked out Gibson for eight weeks. Hughes went 7–2 in his absence and continued to start in the World Series, but a shoulder injury the following year destroyed his career.

One hot streak vaulted the Redbirds into the pennant race, and another ended it. They won fifteen of seventeen games in June to vault

Steve Carlton landed on two all-star teams with the Cardinals before an ill-fated trade to Philadelphia.
PHOTO COURTESY OF THE BASEBALL HALL OF FAME AND MUSEUM

atop the National League before losing fourteen of twenty-three. They were tied for first place on July 24 when they began an 11–1 tear and never let go. Included were seven victories in eight games against fellow contenders Chicago and Cincinnati. St. Louis allowed just two runs per game during that stretch despite the loss of Gibson as Carlton, Hughes, veteran Ray Washburn, and emerging rotation mate Nelson Briles dominated opposing hitters.

The Cardinals would have been considered the surprise club in the World Series given their comparative struggles the previous two seasons. But the Red Sox, who finished ninth in 1966, gained that distinction when they emerged from a torrid, four-team scrum in the American League. What followed was among the fiercest battles in baseball history, from which Gibson emerged with a well-deserved reputation as the greatest big-game pitcher in the sport.

He established his dominance in the opener by striking out nine in the first five innings and continuing to retire Red Sox the rest of the way in a taut 2–1 victory. The Fat Lady sang in the first inning of Game 4, when the Cardinals supported Gibson with four runs. He did not allow the big lead that ballooned to 6–0 to weaken his resolve. He mowed down one of the premier lineups in baseball without allowing more than one baserunner in any inning for the shutout and a 3–1 series lead.

The Sox refused to let their Impossible Dream season die. The sizzling Lonborg won Game 5, then Hughes surrendered four home runs in an 8–4 Game 6 defeat. Boston manager Dick Williams controversially returned his ace to the mound on two days' rest for the winner-take-all finale before a packed-out crowd at Fenway Park. The anticipated pitchers' duel never materialized. Though Brock, Maris, and Julian Javier finished off brilliant series performances by combining for six hits, Gibson clinched its MVP award by fanning ten in a complete-game victory and even slamming a hanging Lonborg slider over the wall in the fifth. His performance had marveled one and all.

Most significantly at the time, however, it fulfilled the deep desire of the Cardinals to stick it to the Boston media and to Williams, all of whom had angered them during the course of the event. Bitterness reigned between the two teams throughout. Reporters covering the

Red Sox, who had lambasted the club in previous years for underperforming, had jumped on the bandwagon and trashed the Cardinals as the Fall Classic approached. One paper even accused the wives of St. Louis players of draping mink coats over their chairs at games so Sox wives could not sit down. Another offered that aside from Gibson, the Cardinals were losers.

The bashing continued, leading Brock to claim after that series that he no longer paid attention. "I stopped reading the Boston papers and what their players were supposed to be saying about us three days before the end of the thing," he said. "There is an element of professionalism in baseball that should not be violated. Once you start saying you're going to beat the other guy, you better do it or you're asking for it."[3]

Among the comments to which Brock referred was uttered by Williams, who, when asked about his lineup before Game 7, proclaimed, "Lonborg and champagne." The declaration was splashed in a blaring red headline on the front page. Meanwhile, Red Sox slugger George Scott predicted Gibson would not last five innings—quite a boast given the previous dominance of the right-hander. "That about did it," said Maxvill. "After that, we weren't playing one game for the three thousand dollars between winning and losing shares. We never wanted to beat anybody all year long as much as we wanted to beat them in the seventh game."[4]

Busch was not about to tinker with a winning formula. Professional differences motivated him to reassign Musial as the general manager and return Bing Devine to that post. But both the starting lineup and the rotation remained identical to start the 1968 season. And though the production of several hitters declined, and the Cardinals scored 112 fewer runs than they had in 1967, the difference was offset by the weakening of nearly all offenses in baseball in the Year of the Pitcher. And the staff, led by the now-incomparable Gibson, again displayed its talent and depth. The veteran Washburn, whose curveball baffled hitters from start to finish and even tossed the first St. Louis no-hitter in twenty-seven years against San Francisco on September 18, excelled in his best season before faltering.

The Redbirds seemingly traversed the same path to the NL crown they had a year earlier. They bolted to the top, struggled in May, losing

Red Schoendienst managed the Cardinals to the crown in 1967, and even made cameos with the club in 1980 and 1990.

PHOTO COURTESY OF THE BASEBALL HALL OF FAME AND MUSEUM

eleven of thirteen at one point, then turned on the jets. They snagged first place on June 2 and spent two and a half months increasing their lead. A second straight World Series berth had become a foregone conclusion by mid-July.

Their Fall Classic foe was no young upstart as had been the Red Sox. The Detroit Tigers, featuring one breakout batting star in Willie Horton and such veteran standouts as catcher Bill Freehan, first baseman Norm Cash, and outfielder Al Kaline, awaited. The runaway winners of the American League also promised to match St. Louis pitch for pitch with a rotation featuring Denny McLain, perhaps the last thirty-game winner ever, Earl Wilson, and Mickey Lolich.

Those who anticipated scintillating pitching duels between Gibson and McLain were sorely disappointed. Only Gibson performed to his standards. He proved even more dominant than in the previous World Series in allowing just one run in Game 1 and Game 4 combined with twenty-seven strikeouts. But aside from one strong effort by Washburn in Game 3, his fellow starters failed to tame the Tigers. Washburn collapsed in a ten-run third inning in Game 6 with a chance to clinch the crown, leaving it up once again to Gibson to save the day. And when he finally faltered—greatly due to Flood's fielding miscue in the seventh inning—the Cardinals were doomed.

Recalled Gibson in his autobiography about the critical play in which Flood charged in and allowed the Jim Northrup line drive to soar over his head, "As soon as the ball left the bat, I was confident Flood would track it down, and he had done on so many similar occasions over the years. This time, though, Curt's first step was toward the infield, and when he realized he had underestimated the hit, he turned sharply, and for a split second lost his footing on the wet grass."[5]

World Series hero Mickey Lolich did the rest, shutting St. Louis down, earning the ultimate distinction of outpitching McLain and Gibson, and earning MVP honors. An era of greatness was over and one of inconsistency and only occasional contention was about to begin.

CHAPTER FIFTEEN

Flying High, but Not Soaring

MAJOR LEAGUE BASEBALL DETERMINED AFTER THE 1968 SEASON THAT a lack of action in the sport and diminishing popularity necessitated changes. It added two expansion franchises in both leagues and created a four-division setup. Mounds were lowered to weaken pitching dominance and promote more run production. The game had grown dull to the average fan.

The new emphasis on offense and power left the Cardinals behind in 1969. They had in March swapped one slugging first baseman for another when they sent Orlando Cepeda to Atlanta for veteran Joe Torre, who led the team with eighteen home runs and 101 RBI. But that was the problem. No other St. Louis hitter managed more than twelve home runs as the club finished last in the National League in that category and a mere tenth in runs scored. Too often table setters Brock and Flood were left stranded on base.

Brilliant pitching from Gibson and Carlton, who performed as if unaffected by the lower mound, allowed the Cardinals to remain strong. Rookie right-hander Mike Torrez caught fire in mid-July to win his last nine decisions, and he remained hot early in 1970 before fading and getting dealt to Montreal for nondescript pitcher Bob Reynolds in 1971. It was a trade GM Bing Devine would sorely regret when Torrez blossomed into a consistent winner.

Even dynamite pitching could not have saved the 1969 Cardinals, particularly early in the season. They scored three runs or fewer in twenty-one of their first thirty games in stumbling to a 12–18 record and falling

7.5 games out of first place by May 11. They performed better thereafter, but sizzling stretches by the Cubs, then the Miracle Mets, prevented them from vaulting back into contention.

Continuity could not save the Cardinals during that era. The combination of Devine and Hall of Fame manager Red Schoendienst, whose first tenure at the helm lasted twelve years, resulted after 1968 in mostly winning records but only one foray into a pennant race in 1974. Not that Devine merely twiddled his thumbs—he toiled in vain to improve the roster.

Sometimes circumstances pushed against him. Among them was the relationship between the organization and Flood, which soured in 1969. Flood had demanded a $90,000 salary after what he considered a demeaning offer of a $5,000 raise to $77,500. Personal problems also haunted Flood, who had taken in his brother Carl, who had been out on parole after being imprisoned for bank robbery. Soon thereafter, Carl and an accomplice tried to rob a jewelry store and led the police on a car chase through downtown St. Louis. The highly publicized event irked Cardinals management.

Owner Gussie Busch exacerbated tensions with Flood by gathering franchise bigwigs and the media during spring training in 1969 for a lecture to the players. Busch sermonized that his charges should be motivated less by personal greed and more by wanting to improve performance on the field and develop stronger relationships with the media and fans. Flood believed the admonishment was directed more at him than anyone else, but he believed it had a negative effect on the entire club.

"In 1969, we lost the championship of the National League on March 22 before the season started," Flood offered in his 1971 book, entitled *The Way It Is*. "I feared that if I so much as hinted at the truth about that meeting I would be gone from the team in a week. I was sick with shame and so was everyone else on the Cardinals. . . . The speech demoralized the 1969 Cardinals. . . . We became a morose and touchy team."[1]

Flood, who soon lost his position as co-captain of the club, became further rankled when he was fined $250 in May for missing a public function—never mind he had been spiked on the field the previous night and was in pain. And with the Cardinals doomed to a middle-of-the-pack finish in August, several players complained to the media about Schoendienst benching veterans in favor of rookies. Devine assumed that Flood was leading the charge.

The die was cast. Less than a week after the regular season concluded, Devine traded Flood and McCarver to the struggling Phillies most notably for first baseman Richie Allen, a fellow malcontent who had worn out his welcome with that organization. Flood was devastated. He loved the city of St. Louis, his teammates, and the fans. And he was not enamored with his new destination. He wrote the following in his book:

> Philadelphia. The nation's northernmost southern city, scene of Richie Allen's ordeals. Home of a ballclub rivaled only by the Pirates as the least cheerful organization in the league. When the proud Cardinals were riding a chartered jet, the Phils were still lumbering through the air in propeller jobs, arriving on the Coast too late to get proper rest before submitting to murder by the Giants and Dodgers. I did not want to succeed Richie Allen in the affections of that organization, its press and its catcalling, missile-hurling audience.[2]

Even a salary offer of $100,000 from Phillies GM Bob Quinn failed to sway Flood. He was stuck between a rock and a hard place. He did not want to retire, but the reserve clause prevented him from selling his services to the highest bidder. So, he embarked on his historical challenge that, despite its initial failure in the Supreme Court, eventually led to the advent of free agency. His playing career was destroyed, but his impact on the sport and its positive effect for players proved far more consequential.

The refusal of Flood to report to Philadelphia forced St. Louis to send promising outfielder Willie Montanez instead. The wheeling and dealing were not catastrophic for the Cardinals, but they certainly damaged their offense beyond the one season Allen played in St. Louis. He began with a bang in 1970 with a homer and two doubles in a win at Montreal and piqued the excitement of fans. A crowd of 45,790 turned out for his home debut on April 10 and gave him a standing ovation—quite a change from the boos he'd regularly heard at his old venue.

Allen was pacing the club in home runs and RBI in mid-August when he tore a hamstring sliding into second base. Though Devine and Schoendienst denied accusations that they believed he had milked his recovery, he played just five more games and was traded to the Dodgers four days after the season concluded for weak-hitting second baseman Ted Sizemore, ostensibly to improve their defense at that position with Julian Javier aging. Two years later, Allen won American League MVP honors with the White Sox. The Redbirds in the meantime maintained their troubling status as one of the poorest power-hitting teams in baseball.

While the Cardinals struggled to find rotation help for the still-effective Gibson, in the early 1970s their offense rode a roller coaster from one year to the next. The blossoming of young catcher Ted Simmons in 1971 added a consistent and productive bat to the lineup, and Brock, like a fine wine, seemed to get better with age, leading the senior circuit in stolen bases eight times in nine years and capping off his incredible run with what remained through 2021 an NL-record 118 thefts in 1974. But the team was too dependent on Torre for power. The Cardinals ranked second in runs scored when he blasted twenty-four home runs and drove in 137 in 1971 to earn MVP honors. But they struggled to score over the next few years when he experienced a power outage.

Far more damaging was an ill-fated trade of Carlton to Philadelphia for right-hander Rick Wise early in spring training 1972. The deal for Wise appeared wise enough when Devine engineered it, given their track records. The two compared evenly in age, experience, and a wide array of statistical categories through that year. Wise had even outperformed Carlton in 1971. The impetus of the swap was a contentious salary dispute between Carlton and Cardinals management that was ironed out in 1970, but it eventually motivated the GM to unload the lanky lefty. "I don't care if he ever pitches a ball for us again," Devine declared that March after Carlton turned down his contract offer. He also expressed his disappointment with Carlton to the *Sporting News*, adding, "I don't like his attitude, not a damn bit."[3]

Carlton eventually signed a two-year deal for $80,000. Devine later claimed that Busch wanted him gone. The emotions of the hierarchy resulted in the departure of a pitcher who would win 252 more games in the big leagues and four Cy Young Awards. Included were twenty-seven victories in 1972 for a terrible Phillies club in one of the most remarkable years crafted by any pitcher in baseball history. Wise performed to expectations, winning thirty-two games in two seasons for St. Louis and earning an All-Star game nod in 1973. But Carlton proved downright otherworldly.

The Redbirds stumbled along inconsistently well into the decade and required one weak season from their National League East foes to slide into contention in 1974. Riding the 118 steals from Brock, speedy outfielder and Rookie of the Year Bake McBride and tightly wound blossoming closer Al Hrabosky, as well as the bats of Simmons and veteran outfielder Reggie Smith, who was acquired from Boston for Wise, and young outfielder Bernie Carbo, the club remained in the race throughout.

They appeared likely to snag the division crown after concluding a six-game winning streak on September 16. But two losses at second-place Pittsburgh and two more at home against the Pirates allowed that team to take over the lead. The Cardinals battled back to forge a first-place tie, with one game remaining against lowly Montreal. Gibson seemed destined to rise to the occasion yet again when he pitched the club to a 2–1 lead heading into the eighth inning, but a Mike Jorgensen home run doomed St. Louis to defeat and elimination. "What can I say?" Schoendienst exclaimed in the downcast locker room after the game. "I was thinking about bringing in Hrabosky, but Gibby was pitching so well."[4]

The inevitable downfall of Gibson the next season doomed St. Louis to mediocrity and eventually resulted in the departure of Schoendienst and Devine. They had launched a youth movement in their rotation featuring talents such as Bob Forsch, Lynn McGlothen, and John Denny, all of whom performed well as Bullet Bob finally reached the end. Denny even earned the National League ERA title in 1976. But the pitched staff lacked depth, and the offense was practically devoid of power. The Cardinals managed just sixty-three home runs that season and lost ninety games for the first time since 1916.

Citing the need for a new direction, Busch fired Schoendienst immediately following the season. Despite having failed to reach the playoffs since 1968, the skipper recalled his surprise in his book, *Red: A Baseball*

Life, when the word of his dismissal came down. "It caught me a little off guard," he wrote. "The organization decided to make changes. It was as simple as that, and there was really no argument I could make. I never second-guessed myself. I never regretted any move or decision I made, and I was happy with the job I had done."[5]

Busch believed the players required more discipline than the easygoing Schoendienst preferred. So, he hired minor league manager Vern Rapp, who had succeeded at the helm of Triple-A Denver and had certainly steered the ship in the opposite direction. He even demanded that colorful closer Al Hrabosky shave off his signature "Fu Manchu" moustache. Hrabosky felt his persona positively affected his mindset and his performance on the mound, later claiming that the loss of his facial hair made him feel "like a soldier going to war without his rifle." He demanded a trade after one season under Rapp.[6]

Though St. Louis rebounded to finish over .500 in 1977, greatly due to the continued slugging of Simmons and the blossoming of young first baseman Keith Hernandez, the rotation was a mess beyond twenty-game winner Bob Forsch. The Cardinals collapsed down the stretch, and the unpopularity of Rapp carried over into the following season. Busch wasted little time firing him after a 6–11 start, eventually replacing him with former St. Louis playing star Ken Boyer.

The club was a mess. Brock was approaching forty and finally faltering at the plate, Hernandez had temporarily regressed, and though young pitchers such as Pete Vuckovich, Denny, and Forsch formed a decent trio, they did not receive enough run support to win consistently. The team bottomed out at 69–93 in 1978. And Devine was fired for the second time. He was replaced by John Claiborne, whom Devine had originally hired as an assistant more than a decade earlier. Devine later successfully recommended Claiborne for a scouting director job with Oakland before the latter moved to Boston as a scout and helped the Red Sox win the 1975 American League pennant.

Personal and personnel matters grew complex when Busch hired Claiborne to take over for Devine, who was offered a consulting position under the new GM. "I thought Bing would accept it because of (Clai-

Keith Hernandez and his sweet swing had some big years with the Cardinals.
PHOTO COURTESY OF DREAMSTIME

borne's) friendship with Mr. Devine," Busch said. Offered Devine: "He underestimated the self-esteem in which I hold myself."[7]

Though the Cardinals rebounded from mediocrity in the second half of the 1979 season, Boyer was not long for the job. Neither was Claiborne. A slow start in 1980 prompted Busch to can Boyer, and Claiborne was summarily dismissed that summer. The revolving door was spinning rapidly in St. Louis. The beneficiary was Missouri favorite Whitey Herzog, who had worn out his welcome with the Kansas City Royals after managing that club to five consecutive winning seasons. Herzog took

Long-haired catcher Ted Simmons—nicknamed "Simba"—was a stalwart for the Cardinals throughout the 1970s.
PHOTO COURTESY OF THE BASEBALL HALL OF FAME AND MUSEUM

over for Boyer before a promotion to general manager when Claiborne received his pink slip. And in the ultimate irony, he was replaced in the dugout by none other than Schoendienst.

The Cardinals performed far better offensively under Herzog and Schoendienst than they had with Boyer running the show. They had established an offense that would soon prove ideal for the artificial turf at Busch Stadium. They still lacked power, though veteran outfielder George Hendrick, a trade steal from San Diego, provided twenty-five home runs and 109 RBI in 1980. But they led the league with a whopping three hundred doubles and were about to take their new style to another level.

Chapter Sixteen

The Powerless Wonders

FOR GENERATIONS SINCE BABE RUTH OBLITERATED THE DEAD BALL ERA by slugging prodigious clouts over fences in American League ballparks, the assumption was that teams required at least a modicum of power to contend. The early-1980s Cardinals were about to destroy that theory.

Herzog, who had moved his friend Schoendienst back to a coaching position after the 1980 season, went to work as the first GM in major league baseball since Connie Mack ruled the roost with the Philadelphia Athletics in 1950. Herzog busily set about reconstructing the roster to fit his managing philosophies and continue to maximize the benefits of playing at Busch Stadium, though one of his first moves was acquiring super closer and split-finger fastball master Bruce Sutter from the Cubs for young power-hitting first baseman Leon Durham, who went on to thrive in Chicago but was stuck behind Keith Hernandez in St. Louis. Sutter led the league in saves three times over the next four years and finished among the top five in Cy Young Award voting after each of those seasons.

The full potential of the evolving Cardinals became one of the great unknowns of baseball in 1981. A midseason players strike forced a two-half setup during which they managed a 59–43 record but finished behind the Phillies and Expos, respectively, to lose a playoff opportunity. Herzog then worked in earnest to promote and trade for talent that would raise his team to greatness. He ripped off the Yankees, swapping pitcher Bob Sykes for fleet and promising outfielder Willie McGee. He sent mediocre starting pitchers Sylvio Martinez and Lary Sorensen out in a three-team deal that landed speedy, high-average outfielder Lonnie Smith. And most importantly, he traded fading outfielder Sixto Lezcano and swapped shortstops, dispatching still-in-his-prime Garry Templeton for Ozzie Smith.

The immensely talented Templeton was a steady performer but so volatile that on August 26, 1981, during a "Ladies Day" game at Busch Stadium, he gave the fans the middle-finger salute after they booed him for failing to run to first base on a passed ball. Templeton later repeated the act and grabbed his crotch before being tossed from the game. Herzog bolted onto the field and furiously yanked Templeton into the dugout. "I don't think Templeton has the guts to apologize to the rest of us," said teammate Gene Tenace. "He's a loser. We're better off without him. I don't think he'll even be playing two or three years from now."[1]

Templeton played for another decade but never hit as well as he had in St. Louis. Meanwhile, Smith blossomed into a Hall of Famer and arguably the finest defensive shortstop in baseball history. Herzog had constructed his ideal team and felt no need to maintain his role as GM. He handed that job over to assistant Joe McDonald three games into the 1982 season and watched his Cardinals fly from the dugout. They sped around the bases, pacing the senior circuit with fifty-two triples and two hundred stolen bases. Even Hernandez and Hendrick did not require power for production—they combined for just twenty-six home runs but 198 RBI. The style of play embraced by the Cardinals was soon named after their manager.

"Whiteyball was nothing more than playing good, sound, fundamental baseball—baseball the way baseball was supposed to be played," said Smith in 2010. "You knew that if you kept the game close, with your overall team speed and being able to put the ball in play, you could keep pressure on a defense that probably was not as effective as yours. It's real simple. It's not any mathematical equation. It's just about pitching, catching, timely hitting, and keeping pressure on the opposition."[2]

Herzog had not ignored his rotation, which was still led by Forsch, who had established himself as no more than a steady starter. The club desperately needed an ace and had found one the previous summer in right-hander Joaquin Andujar, whom they acquired for expendable outfielder Tony Scott. Andujar was no unknown. He had neared two all-star berths in Houston, but the Astros feared he was fading. Andujar proved them wrong in emerging as the ace of the St. Louis staff.

The results of all the maneuvering were spectacular in 1982. The Cardinals broke from the gate on fire, winning twelve straight games in early April to snag first place. They remained hot into early June to stretch their lead to 5.5 games before faltering a bit and embarking on a nip-and-tuck battle with Philadelphia for the pennant. They beat the Phillies twice on the road, then swept five straight for the Mets in New York to all but clinch the crown. Tremendous pitching keyed the run—St. Louis allowed just eighteen runs in a 10–3 stretch that included four shutouts.

That sterling hurling continued in a 3–0 rout of Atlanta in the division series. Forsch and Andujar dominated the Braves in their outings. The only drama arose in Game 2, which light-hitting third baseman Ken Oberkfell won for St. Louis with a walk-off single after Sutter had displayed his usual brilliance in relief.

The World Series promised a lively clash of opposites. On deck were the offensive juggernaut Milwaukee Brewers, who bashed foes into oblivion with such sluggers as NL MVP Robin Yount, Paul Molitor, Ben Oglivie, Cecil Cooper, and Gorman Thomas. They even featured two former St. Louis standouts in catcher Ted Simmons and AL Cy Young Award winner Pete Vuckovich (whose 1.502 WHIP would certainly have disqualified him for the honor in the modern era).

And when they bludgeoned Forsch in the opener, it appeared the team known as Harvey's Walllbangers—named after Milwaukee manager Harvey Kuenn—could overwhelm Whiteyball with its daunting lineup. But former Brewer catcher Darrell Porter played hero in Game 2 to tie the series. He threw out Molitor trying to steal in the ninth to secure the first out, and Sutter did the rest in a 5–4 victory.

Andujar planted the seeds of his series greatness in Game 3 as McGee untypically blasted two home runs, but the vaunted Wallbangers could not be muted for long. They exploded for six runs in the seventh inning to overcome a 5–1 deficit for the Game 4 victory, then beat Forsch again the next night to place themselves on the verge of their first championship.

Whitey Herzog won it all in 1982 before managing the Cardinals to the brink of two more World Series crowns.
PHOTO COURTESY OF DREAMSTIME

The Cardinals returned home with their backs against the wall. Rookie right-hander John Stuper, who had arrived in early June and performed consistently in the rotation, handcuffed Milwaukee on four hits while his teammates slammed out thirteen runs on twelve hits, including three from surprising World Series hero and typical reserve Dane Iorg.

The result was one clash for the crown. Milwaukee forged ahead 3–1 against Andujar, but St. Louis used its offensive style to overcome the deficit. Run-scoring singles by Hernandez and Hendrick provided the lead in the sixth and two more from Porter and hitting specialist Steve Braun stretched the lead to 6–3. With Sutter on the mound in the ninth, it was all over but the celebration. He fanned Thomas on a high 3–2 fastball to end it, prompting Hall of Fame Cardinals radio announcer Jack Buck to exclaim, "A swing and a miss, and that's a winner! A World Series winner for the Cardinals!" About 150 police officers could not stop the fans from climbing over the walls and rushing the field.[3]

"It was the most fun I've had playing baseball in my whole career," offered Porter in the jubilant locker room, adding that after the Cardinals fell behind in Game 7, "We weren't afraid. We felt like we had a good chance to come back."[4]

They also felt like they had a good chance to come back and win another pennant in 1983, but instead they plummeted back to earth with virtually the same cast. Whereas they thrived despite a lack of home run hitters in 1982, the continued power outage proved far more damaging the following year. Hernandez suffered from cocaine addiction, motivating McDonald to trade him to the Mets in June, forcing Hendrick to move to first base and limiting the offense. Meanwhile, Forsch, Andujar, and Sutter all regressed significantly as the Cardinals finished near the bottom of the league in team ERA. They remained in the pennant race into September in a woefully weak division despite playing .500 ball, but three-game sweeps in Philadelphia and Montreal eventually doomed them to a fourth-place finish.

The stunning and sudden decline of Stuper, and back problems that sent Forsch reeling, left twenty-game winner Andujar as the lone dependable starter in 1984. Sutter saved a career-high forty-five that year but might have reached sixty without the limited opportunities. A strengthened division precluded any chance for the Redbirds to remain in the race—they were cooked by mid-July. The bloom was off the rose, and few gave hope that a rebound to greatness was on the horizon. Busch was among the skeptical. He forced McDonald to resign as GM and replaced him with former St. Louis shortstop Dal Maxvill, who interviewed for the job on the owner's yacht, took a walk on the beach, then learned of his hiring on a one-year basis. Busch was taking no chances.

No sweat. Maxvill recognized the talent within the organization and refused to make sweeping changes. Among the young standouts was blurry fast outfielder Vince Coleman, who struck out far too much for a

Slap hitter Willie McGee wreaked havoc at the plate and on the bases for the Cardinals of the 1980s.
PHOTO COURTESY OF DREAMSTIME

slap hitter but who reached base enough to drive opponents crazy. He set a major league rookie record with 110 stolen bases in 1985 as his team recorded 312 thefts, the most in the National League since 1912. The Cardinals had reestablished their 1982 style. They ranked second-to-last in home runs, but first in runs scored by slamming doubles and stealing bases. Most notable was second baseman Tommy Herr, who racked up 110 RBI despite sending just eight over the fence, and McGee, who ripped off fifty-six bases, paced the league with eighteen triples and a .353 average, and captured Most Valuable Player honors.

McDonald contributed greatly in December before his dismissal. He sent Hendrick to Pittsburgh for heretofore mediocre southpaw John Tudor, who blossomed in St. Louis with a 21–8 record and glistening 1.93 ERA to place second in the Cy Young Award voting. His ten shutouts led the league. Tudor, Andujar, and Britain native Danny Cox, who faded fast after three strong seasons, combined for sixty victories. The Cardinals didn't even miss free agent defection Sutter. A bullpen by committee led by one-year wonder Jeff Lahti ensured that winnable games were not lost. McDonald also supplemented a meager power source by swapping several mediocrities to San Francisco for slugging first baseman Jack Clark.

The 1985 club did not mesh immediately. It appeared destined to fail in mid-May with a 16–19 record and fourth-place standing. But the Redbirds heated up in June and stayed hot. The consistent winning would have typically blown away the competition, but the vastly talented Mets refused to die. They beat the Cardinals twice before huge crowds at Busch Stadium to cut their deficit to one game. A throng of 47,720 packed the place for the finale of the series that could have eliminated the St. Louis lead in the division. Keith Hernandez tried to torture his former teammates by slamming five hits. But Cox overcame a horrible first inning that threatened to knock him out as his team survived. Tudor beat the Cubs two days later to clinch the NL East crown.

Several days later, it seemed the playoff nightmare had followed the dream season. The offense had been smothered under the weight of a stupendous pitching staff in the first two games of the NLCS in Los Angeles. Led by hurling heavyweights Fernando Valenzuela and Orel Hershiser, the Dodgers staff had allowed an average of seven hits per game in 1985, and that pair thoroughly outpitched Tudor and Andujar. But the offense flipped a switch and swept three in St. Louis.

The most dramatic moment arrived in the ninth inning of Game 5 when Ozzie Smith, who had managed a career-high six home runs all year, stepped to the plate against tough Dodgers right-hander Tom Niedenfuer. Smith yanked a fastball over the fence down the right-field line, prompting Buck to shout one of the most famous calls in baseball history: "Go crazy, folks! Go crazy!"[5]

The Cardinals gave their patrons a chance to go crazy again two nights later. This time Clark played the role of hero against series goat Niedenfuer, blasting a three-run homer with two out in the ninth to turn a 5–4 deficit into a 7–5 victory. Los Angeles manager Tommy Lasorda considered walking Clark with struggling Andy Van Slyke on deck and

Ozzie Smith—the Wizard of Oz—was arguably the greatest defensive shortstop in the history of the sport.

PHOTO COURTESY OF DREAMSTIME

first base open but decided against it. And as the ball soared over the left-field fence, Dodgers left fielder Pedro Guerrero slammed his glove to the ground in disgust.

Clark enjoyed that scene. He had been tortured enough by LA pitching over the years playing with the rival Giants. He even felt a strong dislike for Lasorda and Dodger fans. "There was a lot of payback for a lot of reasons," he said years later. "For all those years in Candlestick Park. Not only was it bad enough just having to play there, but the Dodgers kept whipping up on us every year. I had one mission: to seek and destroy everyone on that team, from Fernando to Orel Hershiser. I wanted it all. I tried to hit it out of the stadium. I didn't just want a home run. I wanted to have it be shot out of a cannon."[6]

The tables turned on the Cardinals in a Missouri-pride World Series against Kansas City. They seemed destined to capture their second crown in four years when Tudor delighted a sellout crowd at Busch with a five-hit shutout in Game 4 to place his team on the brink of a championship. But the club collapsed offensively thereafter. They scored just two runs the rest of the way and managed a mere five hits in each of the last three games. It appeared they would overcome their futile batsmen when Cox and Ken Dayley combined to blank Kansas City through eight innings in Game 6. But a notoriously bad call by first-base umpire Don Denkinger allowed leadoff hitter Jorge Orta to reach as Herzog angrily objected. Previously unhittable rookie reliever Todd Worrell, who would emerge as a dynamite closer in future seasons, allowed another hit before—in a case of dripping irony—1982 St. Louis World Series hero Dane Iorg looped a broken-bat, two-run single to snatch victory from the jaws of defeat for the Royals.

The devastated Cardinals could not recover. Herzog virtually predicted defeat with Denkinger calling balls and strikes in Game 7 following their argument the night before. "As far as I'm concerned, we had the damned World Series won tonight," he said. "We've got no more chance of winning (Game 7) than the man in the moon—not with that guy working behind home plate."[7]

Kansas City ace Bret Saberhagen didn't need any assistance. He received all the help required when his mates knocked Tudor out in the third inning in an 11–0 rout. The title that was so enticingly close had been grabbed away from the Cardinals. They would have to wait twenty-one years to celebrate another one.

Despite the World Series crowns it has won, arguably the greatest franchise in National League history cannot be judged on them, but rather on its consistency. But a rare stretch of inconstancy did follow the disappointing conclusion of the 1985 Fall Classic.

CHAPTER SEVENTEEN

The Yo-Yo Years

GAME 7 OF THE 1985 WORLD SERIES DID NOT END WITHOUT FIRE-
works that would have a negative effect on the team's immediate future.
Co-ace Joaquin Andujar, who arrived on the mound with the Cardinals
trailing 9–0 and doomed to defeat, lost emotional control in an angry and
embarrassing verbal and nearly physical attack against home plate umpire
Don Denkinger over perceived missed calls, leading to his ejection and
that of manager Whitey Herzog. Those were the last pitches Andujar
threw in a St. Louis uniform. He was traded to Oakland for left-hander
Tim Conroy and backup catcher Mike Heath two months later.

Andujar managed one decent season for the Athletics before fading
away. The failure of Conway or anyone else to replace him in the rotation
hurt the club in 1986. But it was an anemic offense that destroyed St.
Louis that season. The team had shown it could win without blasting
balls over fences. But this power outage proved too great to overcome.
The 1986 Redbirds hit just fifty-eight home runs, one of the lowest totals
of any team in baseball since 1960 and their lowest 162-game season
total through 2021. They ranked last in the league with a .327 on-base
percentage, which precluded any opportunity to score consistently
despite the 107 stolen bases from Vince Coleman. The Cardinals suffered
a severe blow when lone power hitter Jack Clark missed the last four
months with a thumb injury, but a stunning 9–26 stretch that preceded
his loss had long destroyed their chances at a repeat.

The offense of that era indeed walked a tightrope with little margin
for error and fell off in 1986. But it traversed with the talent of a tight-

rope-walker performer the next season. All fell back into place. Clark returned to health for his finest year. His baseball-best 139 walks and .436 on-base percentage reflected the fear pitchers felt upon his approach to the plate, but he swung the bat often enough to lead the team with thirty-five home runs and 106 RBI. McGee emerged for the first time as a major run-producer with 105 RBI, while Pendleton blossomed as well, batting .286 with ninety-six driven in. Even brilliant defensive shortstop

Slugger Jack Clark nearly won NL MVP honors in 1987 after two disappointing seasons with the Cardinals.
PHOTO COURTESY OF DREAMSTIME

Ozzie Smith upped his offensive game by batting .303. The result was 197 more runs scored than in 1986, which allowed for a rather significant weakening on the mound.

The Redbirds wasted no time reestablishing themselves as not only a contender, but a favorite to capture the NL East. A 22–8 blitz in May and June stretched their lead to six games, then another tear into late July stretched it to ten. It appeared they had overcome the absence of Tudor, who broke his leg in April slamming into the St. Louis dugout sprinting after a foul ball and did not return until August.

Then they collapsed. A four-game sweep in San Francisco started a terrible stretch that ended with three straight losses in Houston. Their 9–18 mark during that period shrank their lead to 2.5 games with the Mets and Expos closing in. That is when Tudor returned to play the role of hero. He received plenty of run support but also pitched well enough to win his last seven decisions as the Cardinals overcame a three-game sweep in Montreal to stave off both clubs, finally clinching by taking three of four against the Expos before sellout crowds at Busch.

That set up a pennant battle against a remarkably similar club, though the Giants hit for decidedly more power. Both boasted a slugging star named Clark—twenty-three-year-old Will also bashed thirty-five home runs for San Francisco. Both featured deep lineups with few stars. And neither had anything close to an ace pitcher despite the Giants owning the lowest ERA in the National League.

The taut battle that followed reflected that sameness. Heroes anew emerged every game. The Cardinals' flash-in-the-pan southpaw Greg Mathews won the opener with his arm and bat, stretching the lead to 5–2 with a two-run single. Giants lefty Dave Dravecky blanked the Redbirds on two hits the next night. A flock of Cardinals contributed to a victorious comeback from a 4–0 deficit in Game 3, but San Francisco returned the favor the following evening with a come-from-behind victory of its own.

The Giants seemed likely to deliver the final blow when in Game 5 they destroyed the struggling Forsch, who had been moved to the bullpen. But St. Louis pitchers rose to the occasion. Tudor outperformed Dravecky in a taut 1–0 victory at Busch to set up the all-or-nothing Game 7. That is when a new offensive hero emerged. Jack-of-all-trades singles hitter Jose Oquendo keyed a four-run second inning with a three-run homer, and Cox did the rest, hurling the team's second consecutive shutout to send his team into another World Series. "Was I stunned?" Pendleton replied when asked about the Oquendo blast. "Weren't you?" Added Herzog: "It was a goddamn Christmas present."[1]

Some considered Minnesota easy pickings for the Cardinals. The Twins managed just eighty-five wins and finished in the lower half of the American League in both runs scored and team ERA. They had even lost their last five games of the regular season before burying Detroit to reach the Fall Classic. But the pitchers who had performed well against San Francisco were pounded by the Twins—and Forsch continued to take a beating.

The club simply could not overcome the terrible outings. Minnesota averaged ten runs in its three victories leading up to the clincher that pitted Cox against blossoming left-hander Frank Viola. A four-single second gave the Cardinals a 2–0 lead, but they managed just two hits the rest of the way in a 4–2 defeat that set off a raucous celebration in the Metrodome.

Times had changed. No longer could any club tinker simply within the organization and through trades to ensure consistency. Free agency took a toll on St. Louis in 1988. The defection of Clark forced GM Dal Maxvill to try to replace the only home run bat in the lineup a bit more creatively. So, he traded Herr to the same Minnesota team that had beaten them in the Series for Tom Brunansky, who could neither match Clark in the power nor average departments. Maxvill also took a shot in the dark and signed first baseman Bob Horner, the onetime Atlanta slugger and Rookie of the Year who surprisingly had found no takers the year before as a free agent and hightailed it to Japan for one season. Little could Maxvill have imagined that Horner was cooked. Meanwhile, Herr was replaced at second by rookie Luis Alicea, who was not ready for the big leagues and would never hit at a high level.

The pitching staff was also in flux. Tudor and Cox continued to perform well, but neither could stay healthy. The former was traded to the Dodgers for the stretch run in 1988 while an elbow injury shelved the latter until 1991. The rotation instead was led by young left-hander Joe Magrane and inconsistent trade acquisition Jose DeLeon. Neither produced for long.

One light did shine through in 1989. Maxvill had wisely swapped Tudor for four-time all-star first baseman Pedro Guerrero, who at least for that season finally gave the club its offensive replacement for Clark. He batted .311, led the National League with forty-two doubles, and paced the Redbirds with 111 RBI. His contributions and the best years from DeLeon and Magrane in St. Louis uniforms keyed a foray into the pennant race that died in mid-September.

Then it happened. A Redbirds team that had never performed horribly, performed horribly. The team that had not finished last since 1918 finished last in 1990. They had grown old and bad, despite one last fine hurrah from Tudor, whom they signed as a free agent, and the brilliance of right-hander Lee Smith, who like a fine wine had gotten better over the years and was about to establish himself as arguably the greatest closer in franchise history. Though his departure proved only temporary, the collapse cost Herzog his job at midseason. In a moment of self-reflection and criticism, he admitted disappointment in his own efforts. "I feel like I've underachieved," he said. "I can't get the guys to play."[2]

St. Louis official skipper rescuer Red Schoendienst, who had filled the same role ten years earlier, got them to play. But he only took over to

Right-hander closer Lee Smith racked up a combined ninety saves to lead the league in that category in both 1991 and 1992.
PHOTO COURTESY OF THE BASEBALL HALL OF FAME AND MUSEUM

Joe Torre proved himself a better hitter than manager with the Cardinals after managing in the Big Apple.
PHOTO COURTESY OF DREAMSTIME

give Busch time to find a permanent replacement. And that was former Cardinals standout Joe Torre, who had previously managed the Mets and Braves with limited success.

Torre was highly respected among the players as a strong union man who sided with them in labor matters. He felt uncomfortable in the role of management, particularly during the devastating 1994 strike that threatened to wreck the sport. Torre sent the Redbirds flying again, but not to their hoped-for heights. He proved to be an ideal manager for the youth movement launched by the organization that left only the incomparable Ozzie Smith and fading Guerrero in the lineup among the veterans. The Cardinals pinned their hopes on such talented newcomers as third baseman Todd Zeile and outfielders Ray Lankford and Bernard Gilkey, as well as soft-tossing, late-bloomer pitcher Bob Tewksbury, who boasted incredible control and emerged briefly as an ace.

High risers in the NL East during that era, such as Atlanta, Philadelphia, and Montreal, precluded merely good teams such as St. Louis from contending. The Redbirds simply lacked the talent under Torre to keep up. They continued to build their team offensively to fit the fast-playing artificial turf at Busch Stadium, but they could no longer score enough without home run power, particularly in a period in which big boppers had become more prevalent. Only three Cardinals slammed twenty or more home runs in a season from 1988 to 1994, and none managed more than twenty-five. Meanwhile, their deep and talented bullpen, led by Smith, was not enough to overcome a mediocre rotation.

The Cardinals plunged from average to lousy again in 1995, after a shakeup at the top of the organization. Maxvill was fired as general manager by new team president Mark Lampling, who cited a need for change during the midst of the strike that had cost baseball the World Series. Maxvill, who remained on as a part-time scout, was replaced by Walt Jocketty, who had been credited for rebuilding a shattered Oakland farm system to produce such stars as Jose Canseco and Mark McGwire. The latter would eventually and controversially begin to rewrite the St. Louis record books.

Lampling nearly hired Philadelphia GM Lee Thomas. That candidate withdrew himself from consideration, but Lampling claimed that Jocketty might have received the job anyway. The newcomer expressed interest in moving beyond talent evaluation into the modern world of baseball that must be embraced by general managers. "Business fascinates me," Jocketty said. "The general manager's job has evolved to the point where it's not just evaluating talent anymore. You have to be able to run a business."[3]

Among the most vocal Jocketty supporters was Oakland manager Tony La Russa. Jocketty returned the favor by naming La Russa the new Cardinals manager three weeks after a disappointing 1995 season concluded. The offense was a mess beyond the talented outfield triumvirate of Gilkey, Lankford, and super-athletic Brian Jordan, who had played defensive back for the NFL Atlanta Falcons and boasted a deadly combination of power and speed. And the staff desperately needed an ace—only one St. Louis pitcher had won more than seven games in 1995, and that was reliever Rich DeLucia.

Jocketty went to work. The seeds were about to be planted for an era of success far more typical of Redbirds baseball.

CHAPTER EIGHTEEN

New Blood and the Return
of Championship Baseball

TWO MONTHS HAS PASSED SINCE THE CARDINALS HAD CONCLUDED ONE of the worst seasons in franchise history. Only a schedule shortened by the strike that had lasted through the offseason likely prevented them from losing ninety games.

It was two days before Christmas in 1995 when Anheuser-Busch sold the franchise after forty-three years of ownership. The new controllers were a group of investors led by St. Louis lawyer Fred Hanser. Despite fine attendance at various points in its history, rumors persisted that as a small-market club, it could hightail it out of town. But the purchasers assured that the organization would not be moved.

More changes were on the horizon beyond the hiring of La Russa as manager. Rather than commit to a youth movement, with Ozzie Smith and Willie McGee finally fading into the sunset, the club committed $8 million more to its payroll in 1996. The Cardinals spent money in free agency on aging power-hitting third baseman Gary Gaetti. And on the day when they announced the sale of the club, they signed in-his-prime starting pitcher Andy Benes (who joined younger brother Alan in the rotation) and slugging outfielder Ron Gant on the open market.

One and all helped the Redbirds fly right. The Benes brothers combined with trade acquisition Todd Stottlemyre and consistent left-hander Donovan Osborne to form a strong starting quartet, while the offense had finally gained enough power during an era in baseball that required

The Cardinals were a perennial playoff team and two-time World Series champion in sixteen years under manager Tony La Russa.
PHOTO COURTESY OF DREAMSTIME

it to thrive. The foursome of Gaetti, Gant, Lankford, and Jordan averaged twenty-two home runs and ninety RBI between them.

The early results were far from spectacular. Only weak competition in the National League Central, to which the Cardinals moved in 1995, prevented an early slide out of contention. They fell into fifth place at 17–26 in late May but managed a month later to forget a tie for the top despite an under-.500 record. It became clear that any Central club that could string some wins together could capture the crown.

That is what the Redbirds did in late June and July, but the dominance proved only temporary. The race careened into September with seemingly nobody wanting to take the silver platter. A collapse by Houston and Cincinnati that month allowed the Cardinals back into the division title.

St. Louis had won it with short, winning bursts, but its inconsistency did not bode well for the first round of the playoffs against San Diego. Perhaps the most compelling matchup of the series focused on future Hall of Fame closers Trevor Hoffman and Dennis Eckersley, a preseason trade acquisition by the Redbirds who, at the age of forty-two, had found his groove over the previous two months.

It was no contest. Stottlemyre set the tone by performing brilliantly in the opener and allowing Eckersley to record the first of three shutout saves in the best-of-five sweep. And when Hoffman had a chance to keep his team alive, he failed, as Jordan slammed a two-run homer off him in the ninth inning of the clincher.

The defending World Series champion Braves promised far greater resistance with the NL pennant on the line. The Padres boasted nary an ace—Atlanta had three of them with Cy Young Award winner John Smoltz and the incomparable, baffling Greg Maddux leading the way. But the Cardinal bats came alive, even burying Maddux in Game 2. And when Jordan played the role of hero again in Game 4 with a go-ahead blast, and then Eckersley shut the door, they were on the verge of a major upset and World Series berth.

Then a pitching and batting slump arrived at just the wrong time. Stottlemyre and Osborne were crushed with chances to clinch the pennant, and the offense fell into a funk against the best of Braves pitching, scoring just one run in the last three games and none in the finale, a 15–0 defeat in Atlanta recorded at the time as the biggest blowout in major league postseason history. The lone highlight was a pinch-hitting appearance by Smith in the last at-bat of his career.

The man affectionately known as the Wizard of Oz had indeed reached the end of the line. La Russa had even controversially in spring training opened the starting shortstop-position competition between him and young-but-established Royce Clayton, who arrived via trade from San Francisco. The latter claimed the spot, but both performed well at the plate.

St. Louis failed in 1997 to capture that elusive consistently productive offense, a malady that had precluded annual contention. A back injury to Jordan and regression from Gaetti and Gant weakened the offense considerably, leaving only Lankford and fine free agent second baseman Delino DeShields, who led the league in triples and managed his best season, as major producers. The club could not score enough to support promising rookie right-hander Matt Morris and strong rotation mates such as Stottlemyre and the Benes brothers. The Redbirds hung around the periphery of the race in a terribly weak division much of the year before an 8–19 stretch in August destroyed their chances.

But one newcomer wielding a powerful bat that either swished through air at the plate or sent baseballs deep into the night provided hope and excitement. And that was Mark McGwire, for whom the Cardinals traded from Oakland on July 31. The team that day officially joined the Steroid Era Home Run Club. Since the 1994 strike that killed the World Series and disillusioned baseball fans everywhere, the powers-that-be in the sport began promoting the long ball and looking the other way when rumors arose about players using performance-enhancing drugs. The result were threats to the integrity of the game and its most hallowed records.

McGwire hit a ridiculous twenty-four home runs in 174 at-bats after joining the Redbirds in 1997, then embarked on a prodigious long-ball battle with Cubs superstar Sammy Sosa in 1998 that captured the attention of America and helped bring the sport back into the good graces of fans. The era of run-and-stun ball at Busch Stadium was decidedly over—grass had replaced the artificial turf there in 1996. Wins and losses became secondary in St. Louis as the team averaged five runs per game, yet it ranked just sixth offensively in the National League and struggled to find pitching beyond Stottlemyre and Morris, whose arm problems cost him much of the season and soon forced surgery that wiped out his 1999 season.

Burly Mark McGwire embarked on a home-run blitz before becoming one of the leading anti-heroes in the steroid scandal.
PHOTO COURTESY OF DREAMSTIME

The chase to break the single-season home run record of sixty-one held by Roger Maris packed Busch Stadium. The franchise drew more than three million fans despite its mediocrity. The thirty-four-year-old had already mashed fifty-one home runs by August 22, when Associated Press writer Steve Wilstein noticed what he perceived as a suspicious item in McGwire's locker. It was a brown bottle of testosterone-producing androstenedione, which had been banned in the NFL and the Olympics but not by major league baseball. McGwire quickly defended himself to deflect criticism and cited that he was far from alone in using the over-the-counter substance to add power to his game. PEDs in baseball had been thrust into the public eye and would remain a controversial topic for nearly a decade. "Everything I've done is natural," McGwire said when asked about the andro. "Everybody that I know in the game of baseball uses the same stuff I use." McGwire even admitted to using the body-building amino-acid powder creatine.

The race to Maris heated up in September, as neither left much doubt that both would shatter the mark. With five children of the late Maris in the stands and Sosa in right field on September 8, McGwire ripped number sixty-two over the fence down the left-field line before a near-sellout crowd at Busch Stadium against Cubs right-hander Steve Trachsel. And after making it official by reaching home plate, McGwire hoisted his ten-year-old bat-boy son, Matthew, into the air. An eleven-minute celebration followed. "Absolutely incredible." McGwire was beaming that evening. "What can I say? I'm almost speechless. It's been awesome. The last week and a half, my stomach has been turning and my heart beating a million miles a minute. What a feat."[1]

The greatness of that feat has been debated heatedly over the years, given the steroid scandal that followed and rocked baseball. McGwire finished that season with seventy home runs, which remained the all-time record, until San Francisco slugger Barry Bonds, one of many other alleged steroid users of that era, clobbered seventy-three in 2001.

McGwire again exceeded the Maris mark in 1999 and combined with one-year wonder third baseman Fernando Tatis, a trade acquisition from the Rangers, for ninety-nine home runs and 254 RBI. But two offensive standouts and a few other contributors were no longer enough to thrive during the bastardization of the offensive game that had become a reality during the steroid era. The Cardinals placed near the bottom of the league in runs scored despite their production. Only an out-of-the-blue 18–7 season from journeyman right-hander Kent Bottenfield prevented the Cardinals from losing close to one hundred games that year.

The roster required an overhaul, and Jocketty was about to mastermind one. He traded faltering reliever Juan Acevedo to Milwaukee for veteran second baseman and speedy singles hitter Fernando Vina, who for three seasons became a hit machine with St. Louis. He swapped three prospects to the Marlins for multitalented shortstop Edgar Renteria. The two became fixtures at the top of the lineup. Jocketty also unloaded Bottenfield to the Angels at maximum value for Jim Edmonds, a power-hitting center fielder and defensive wonder who regularly made spectacular catches. Edmonds was soon established as the premier threat in the lineup. He batted .295 in 2000 and led the regulars in home runs (forty-two), RBI (110), and on-base percentage (.411). His production offset the loss for most of the year of McGwire, whose chronic knee injury that would end his career prematurely cost him half the season.

Jocketty did not ignore the pitching staff. He took a chance by trading for aging left-hander Darryl Kile, who had taken a chance two years earlier by signing with Colorado and risking his statistics to the rarefied era of notoriously hitter-friendly Coors Field. Kile's ERA soared with the Rockies and resulted in a 21–30 record, but the more spacious confines of Busch Stadium treated him well. He achieved the first twenty-win season for the Redbirds in 2000 since John Tudor and Joaquin Andujar both reached that milestone in 1985. Jocketty also supplemented the broken rotation by trading for former American League Cy Young Award Pat Hentgen. Most stunning, however, was the rapid rise of twenty-year-old prospect pitcher Rick Ankiel, whose career path would take an unusual twist indeed, but not before nearly winning Rookie of the Year honors in 2000.

The Cardinals struck it rich with all the changes. They stormed out of the gate to open a lead in the NL Central, faltered in May, then caught fire to destroy the typically weak division. An interleague defeat of Kansas City on June 6 vaulted them into first place, and there they remained the rest of the year. And they opened the playoffs sizzling hot, having won thirty-two of forty-four at one point down the stretch despite having clinched the crown in mid-September.

A daunting challenge in the Atlanta Braves awaited the offense. Though Hall of Fame pitchers Greg Maddux and Tom Glavine had lost a bit since their glory days of the 1990s, and John Smoltz, who was also bound for Cooperstown, missed the 2000 season with an elbow injury, the Braves staff still presented a difficult task. But the Redbirds soared. They stunned Maddux with a six-run first inning in the opener, then knocked out Glavine in the third inning of Game 2 in delighting sellout crowds at Busch Stadium. The super slugger was Edmonds, who smashed a home run in the first game and three doubles in the second. The series was not over—but it was over. Edmonds blasted another one in a 7–1 win in Atlanta that concluded the destruction.

The Cardinals just kept hitting in the NLCS against the Mets. Even one-year rental Will Clark, who was playing his last major league games, contributed seven hits and a home run. But Kile and Hentgen faltered badly in a five-game defeat. More perplexing and disturbing was the performance of Ankiel, who suddenly, inexplicably lost his control. He had begun his descent with five wild pitches in the third inning of Game 1 against Atlanta, then walked three more in Game 2 of the NLCS before La Russa mercifully removed him. Some dismissed it as the nervousness of youth, but it became symptomatic of a far bigger problem.

"The thing that's most surprising," offered Clark, "is that the last two months, since I've been here, his last eleven starts he's been so dominating. To all of a sudden, out of the clear blue, just lose command the way he has and start throwing his best pitch to the screen, I don't understand that. I've seen guys lose it, left-right, or a little up-down—but not to the point where the catcher needs springs on his shoes."[2]

Aside from the yips that plagued Ankiel, all was well. Young standouts such as J.D. Drew had already arrived, and eventual legend Albert Pujols was waiting in the wings to keep the offense rolling despite the demise of McGwire. Kile and a rejuvenated Morris were set to provide a fine one-two pitching punch. And the turnstiles were turning at a record clip. Fans who had supported the team for generations had gained a reputation as the best in baseball.

CHAPTER NINETEEN

The Finest Fans in the Land

It was October 8, 2021. The Cardinals had, two days earlier, lost the National League wild-card game to Los Angeles, and their season was over. The team released information that understandably brought little attention. But it reflected the growing belief that St. Louis fans were the most passionate in baseball.

The club announced that the local TV ratings topped Major League Baseball that season. That marked the third consecutive year that distinction had been achieved and the twenty-second in a row among the top four. Cardinals baseball had been the number-one primetime show in St. Louis in each of the last twenty nights they played.

Sky-high numbers on the tube did not preclude huge game attendance. The Redbirds ranked in the top-four of National League teams in annual game crowds every season from 1996 through 2021. Only COVID restrictions sent it reeling to under three million in 2021 after sixteen straight seasons exceeding that heady mark.

One might claim, playing devil's advocate, that the lack of an NFL or NBA team, leaving the NHL Blues as the only major sports competition, resulted in greater interest in the Cardinals. But statistics prove different. The team attracted huge numbers while Kurt Warner and Marshall Faulk were leading "The Greatest Show on Turf" Rams to playoff berths and a Super Bowl crown in the late 1990s and early 2000s.

That the Redbirds often joined huge-market clubs such as the Yankees and Dodgers as the only MLB team to average forty thousand fans per game in multiple seasons reflects passion. That their fans have been cited for often cheering great plays made by the opposition proves appreciation for the sport. And the fact that despite temperatures often soaring in St. Louis beyond 90 degrees in the heat of the summer, folks still besiege the ballpark, tells the same story.

The success of the Cardinals on the field over the years can be at least partly attributed to that fan support. Free agents, trade acquisitions, and other players who choose to spend parts of or all their careers in St. Louis have cited that for a significant reason. Among them was sure-to-be Hall of Fame slugger Albert Pujols, who offered, "We've got the best fans in St. Louis. A lot of people come to play in St. Louis because of the way the fans treat us." Pujols even returned to St. Louis to finish his career in 2022 after leaving to sign a massive contract with the Angels, and he was unsurprisingly welcomed back with open arms.[1]

Such loyalty has been traced back to the spirited days of the Gas Houe Gang in the 1930s. But the Cardinals did not arrive as an attendance juggernaut until they generated excitement with the powerless, run-and-stun teams of the early-to-mid-1980s that featured Lonnie Smith, Willie McGee, Tommy Herr, and Vince Coleman. That is when crowds averaging thirty thousand, first seen at Busch during the heady years of 1967 and 1968, returned permanently, with annual figures of three million soon to follow. What legendary St. Louis slugger Stan Musial wrote about fan passion in a book entitled *Cardinals Nation* had become cemented as truth: "Baseball is a religion in St. Louis," Musial stated. "It has always been that way, and I see no reason why that will ever change."[2]

The Redbirds enjoyed an advantage attracting fans during the days of the Gashouse Gang and beyond. Along with the American League St. Louis Browns, whose on-field success and popularity paled in comparison throughout their history until they hightailed it to Baltimore in 1954, they were the westernmost franchise in major league baseball. That allowed them to attract fans from a large region without competition until the Kansas City Royals expanded into existence in 1969. The Cardinal Nation extended throughout the region into Illinois, Arkansas, Iowa, Tennessee, Kentucky, Indiana, and even Oklahoma.

But other factors played more significant roles in the team's popularity. Among them were the legendary figures who connected the club with its fans both before and after the advent of television. The first to capture the imagination of St. Louis fans was legendary pitcher Dizzy Dean, who after a short tenure as coach, which he thoroughly disliked, accepted a job as play-by-play broadcaster of Redbird games on KWK radio. The mere notion excited many—a welcoming committee of three hundred people and a band playing upbeat music greeted him at Union Station as he arrived to start his new gig on July 9, 1941. Dean went on to provide badly needed entertainment with his homespun, conversational style during the war years as the Cardinals emerged as a National League power.

Dean gained fame in the booth for his mangling or altering of the English language. Runners "slud" into second base. Pitchers "throwed" the ball. Batters looked "hitterish" in the box and "swang" at curveballs. Runners halted by a foul ball were forced to return to their "respectable" bases. He understood the attraction of his style and often used it to make valid points. He once said of struggling Red Sox pitcher Mickey Harris, "A pitcher can't throw that way in the majors, or in the minors either, and parade up to the cashiers' window every first and fifteenth."[3]

Dean broadcast games from 1941 to 1946. By the time he left, legendary Harry Caray, who would later become more strongly associated with the Cubs, had begun his quarter century as the voice of the Cardinals. Since there were no exclusive rights to baseball broadcasts at the time, Carey and partner, Gabby Street, competed with Dean early during that period on radio station WIL. The pair gained a faithful following. In 1947, exclusive rights were granted, and Caray's voice was eventually carried to ninety-one stations extending to Mississippi and Oklahoma.

Caray, who later paired with such sportscasting legends as Joe Garagiola and Jack Buck, remained with the club until 1969, when he was fired after rumors surfaced that he had engaged in an affair with Susan Busch, wife of team owner, August. Caray never denied the accusations, claiming wryly that it provided him an ego boost that anyone would believe it was true. He took his schtick and famous home run call ("It might be . . . it could be . . . it IS . . . a home run. . . . Holy cow!") to Chicago, but he would never be considered the most treasured radio or television personality with the Cardinals. That distinction might forever belong to Buck.

Harry Caray earned legend status as a Cardinals broadcaster before leaving for the Windy City.
PHOTO COURTS OF WIKIMEDIA COMMONS

Buck will always be linked to the organization despite having expanded his horizons to work nationally televised games in all four major sports, including seventeen Super Bowls. His passion for baseball began with the crackling of radio broadcasts of any games from which signals could reach his Cleveland home as a teenager. After World War II, during which he received a Purple Heart, he enrolled at Ohio State and began broadcasting its basketball and football games, then landed a job with the Cardinals minor league club in Columbus. Six years later, he was in heady company broadcasting St. Louis games with such luminaries as Caray, Garagiola, and future Braves voice Milo Hamilton. He considered his pairing with Caray as ideal. "When Harry and I were doing the games together, we were as good a team as there ever was," Buck wrote. "His style and mine were so different, that it made for a balanced broadcast. The way we approached the job, with the interest and love both of us had for the game, made our work kind of special."[4]

No broadcaster has been more strongly associated with the Cardinals than the immortal Jack Buck.
PHOTO COURTESY OF THE BASEBALL HALL OF FAME AND MUSEUM

Though Buck quickly branched out, even announcing the legendary 1967 "Ice Bowl" NFL Championship between the Cowboys and Packers, he remained best-known for his strong-voiced, energetic style embraced by fans working the Cardinals and his trademark call on KMOX after the team clinched victory: "That's a winner!"

The firing of Garagiola by owner, August Busch, motivated Buck to recommend broadcasting legend Red Barber as the replacement. But the job went to Jim Woods, who neither appreciated nor attended all the side events the owner wanted him to attend. Two years later, he gave way to former Cardinals third baseman Mike Shannon, who had been forced to retire due to a life-threatening kidney disease. He turned down offers to coach or manage in the minors before eventually accepting an offer to join Buck in the booth in 1972.

That marriage appeared doomed, as well. His fellow broadcasters were taken aback by his performance on the air. "Shannon was raw, raw, raw. Man, he was chopped meat," offered Jay Randolph. Added Ron Jacober: "There were a lot of dissatisfied listeners. I myself wondered how in the world they could have hired this guy. He was just awful." Shannon didn't disagree. He told the *Post-Dispatch* in 1972, "I have a poor radio voice.... I'm not the guy with the golden lungs.... I'll probably be moving out of this business into raising cattle eventually."[5]

Shannon soaked in all he could from his beloved broadcast partner and remained a staple of Redbird broadcasts, eventually taking over for Buck as the lead voice when the latter died in 2002. "I don't know what I would have done without him," Shannon said of Buck. "That man helped me so much. I didn't have to go to broadcasting school—working with Jack was like having a private tutor."[6]

Buck encouraged his student to develop his own style, which he did through distinctive phrases such as his hope-for-a-homer call, "Get up, baby, get up!" But Shannon also had a bit of Yogi Berra in him, blurting out nonsense at any point in a game. After a double by Cardinals hitter Colby Rasmus, he exclaimed, "Woo! He's whistlin' 'round there like he's on his way to the bacon patch!" He described a player as "madder than a pig caught under a barnyard gate." And when one player swung for the fences, Shannon offered: "He was trying to hit a three-run homer with the bases empty. To my knowledge, no one in the history of the game has ever done that. But it could happen someday."[7]

One could not have imagined Shannon remaining in the booth for a half century before finally retiring in 2021. One also could not have imagined Jack Buck's son growing into a Cardinals broadcasting legend as well. Joe Buck took over on the television side in 1991 and remained there through 2007, before emerging as a national figure with Fox Sports and eventually as the lead announcer on *Monday Night Football* games for ESPN.

Many major league teams have featured radio and television broadcasters who never gain fame beyond the cities in which they play. Cardinals broadcast history has for generations maintained and launched some of the greatest careers in the business. They have served as links to what many consider the best baseball fans in America.

The Buck bond was unbreakable. Joe penned a tribute to Jack after the latter died in 2002, including the following: "Millions of baseball fans knew my father, Jack Buck, as the gravelly radio voice of the St. Louis Cardinals. For 40 years, in that funny, folksy, self-deprecating style of his, he had served as the heartland's storyteller, until he had become as beloved as the Cards' most legendary players. At the entrance to Busch Stadium, around the corner from the statue of the great Stan Musial, there is a sculpture of my father holding a microphone. And in Cooperstown, New York, there is a plaque commemorating his election to the National Baseball Hall of Fame.

"But to me he was Dad, my best friend, my hero. I followed him into broadcasting, eventually becoming his partner, calling Cardinals games. Nine years ago, I began a second job telecasting the big national sports events, including the World Series. I was on the road a lot those days, but still I called my dad after every game. I wanted his input and advice. I wanted it still, on this unbearable night. *After you go, Dad, the city will honor you*, I thought. *But what will I do?*"[8]

That is what many St. Louis baseball fans thought when Jack Buck left the broadcast booth for the final time. But those who followed him and the tremendous success of the ballclub in the early days of the twenty-first century helped one and all move on and maintain the enthusiasm and pride about the franchise that the elder Buck had infused in them for decades.

CHAPTER TWENTY

The Early Pujols Years

LITTLE ON THE RÉSUMÉ OF ALBERT PUJOLS SUGGESTED IN 2000 A meteoric rise through the farm system and major league debut at age twenty-one, let alone a unanimous choice as Rookie of the Year and fourth-place standing in the National League Most Valuable Player balloting. After all, the Cardinals had merely plucked him in the thirteenth round of the 1999 draft out of tiny Metropolitan Community College-Maple Woods in Kansas City.

Pujols was angry and disappointed over every major league team passing him up for twelve rounds despite having batted an incredible .466 at the college level with an outrageous twenty-two home runs and seventy-six RBI in 193 at-bats. "I was crying like crazy," Pujols said about his reaction to the draft. "I felt like I did so much, and I didn't get selected in the draft where I knew I could go."[1]

From the first time he displayed his classic swing, plate coverage, and insatiable drive to greatness at Class A Peoria, his destiny appeared on the horizon. Pujols wasted no time launching his rapid ascent toward St. Louis. He batted .324 with just thirty-eight strikeouts in 440 at-bats at that level before moving to advanced Class A, then skipping Double-A and ending the 2000 season by tearing up Triple-A pitching with Louisville.

Such success does not typically guarantee a starting job in the big leagues the following year, but St. Louis manager Tony La Russ and general manager Walt Jocketty had seen enough. Pujols arrived with no set position, but La Russa made certain he found a spot for the young stud in the everyday lineup.

Superstar Albert Pujols played two stints in St. Louis during his Hall of Fame career.
PHOTO COURTESY OF WIKIMEDIA COMMONS

La Russa had challenged Pujols to ensure he was ready. The manager recalled one such test in spring training, when he batted the rookie cleanup against tough Expos right-hander Javier Vazquez. "First time up, he flails at a Vazquez slider well off the plate—looking just terrible—and I think, 'Aha. Got you.' In my mind Albert needs some additional seasoning, he has to work on that small thing—seeing the ball and being better disciplined at the plate. Next time up, Vazquez throws him that same slider and Albert hits a bullet to right-center. I think, 'Holy crap, what an adjustment.'"[2]

Alterations at the plate based on pitching strengths and weaknesses soon became a Pujols trademark. He blossomed quickly into one of the most intelligent hitters in the sport. The rookie played extensively at first base, third base, and in the outfield. He was not merely unaffected by the constant switching but thrived from the jump. Pujols emerged as a sensation in 2001, slamming four home runs in his first eleven games, embarking on a thirteen-game hitting streak and batting .429 through mid-April.

The long drought expected of all first-year players never happened. A mini-slide in early July plunged his average from .354 to .321, but he recovered to finish the season at .329 with forty-seven doubles, thirty-seven home runs, and 130 RBI, a National League record for rookies. Pujols had achieved one of the greatest rookie seasons in baseball history.

That the arrival of Pujols perpetuated the longest run of contention in franchise history is no surprise. He teamed with fellow outfielder Jim Edmonds to create one of the premier hitting tandems in the sport. But it was not until Jocketty added a third wheel to the machine late in 2002

Jim Edmonds was a fine hitter and a spectacular center fielder during his eight seasons in St. Louis.
PHOTO COURTESY OF WIKIMEDIA COMMONS

that the Redbird offense soared to a new level. That was veteran Scott Rolen. The former Phillies standout and Rookie of the Year was traded for fellow third baseman Placido Polanco, who lacked power, fading reliever Mike Timlin, and young southpaw Bud Smith, a highly touted prospect who never lived up to expectations.

Rolen performed brilliantly at the plate and in the field. That he peaked when the Cardinals peaked in wins for a season in 2004 was no coincidence. Their 105 victories represented their highest total since 1944, and the most in franchise history outside the war years. Rolen combined with Pujols and Edmonds to bash 122 home runs and drive in 358. The club led the National League with 855 runs. Meanwhile, a deep pitching staff featuring five strong starters and dynamite closer Jason Isringhausen managed a 3.75 team ERA during the height of the steroid era and gave the Redbirds a chance to win nearly every game.

One pitcher who, despite his advancing years, was considered a surefire rotation mainstay was Darryl Kile. He followed his twenty-win season in 2000 with another fine campaign in which he knocked nearly a point off his ERA. But tragedy struck on June 22, 2002, when Kile never arrived at Wrigley Field for his scheduled start. Security workers at the team hotel broke into his room and discovered he had died in his sleep the night before, after suffering two arterial blockages to his heart. The loss of one of the most respected and hardworking Cardinals stunned his teammates. "Our club is just totally staggered, I mean, devastated," La Russa said. Added Larry Walker: "It's going to be hard to deal with."[3]

The Redbirds struggled for a week following Kile's death before recovering. The staff boasted enough talent and depth to survive. Among those rotation pieces was former Toronto mainstay Chris Carpenter. His performance, which served merely as a prelude to greatness in seasons to come, spotlighted the guile and patience of the front office. Carpenter had appeared washed up two years earlier, the victim of a shoulder injury and expiring contract. Angered by what he considered a slap in the face when the Blue Jays yearned to demote him to Triple-A Syracuse, the right-hander opted to test free agency.

The Cardinals signed him on the cheap with the understanding he would be sidelined until at least July 2003. That move seemed to have backfired when Carpenter took his lumps that summer in his rehab assignments and began feeling discomfort again in the shoulder that had supposedly been patched up by surgery. He even considered retiring—wife, Alyson, talked him out of it—but he chose to undergo another operation to remove scar tissue. Carpenter was sidelined until spring training 2004.

He wasted no time justifying the faith of the organization. Finally healthy in spring training, he displayed the same velocity and command that had made him a steady starter in Toronto. Better yet for the Redbirds, he showed previously unseen late life on his pitches that resulted in more strikeouts and less hard contact. He allowed fewer hits than innings pitched for the first time in his major league career and lowered his WHIP (walks and hits to innings pitched) significantly. The result was a 15–5 record, a 3.46 ERA, and a Sporting News Comeback Player of the Year award.

It was no wonder the Cardinals transformed the NL Central race into a rout. They took over first place on June 11 after a 12–4 surge and continued to increase it. They won an amazing thirty-eight of fifty games during one stretch and coasted to the crown. Two concerns remained. One was a 13–13 finish that stunted their momentum heading into the playoffs. The other was a biceps injury to Carpenter that prevented him from pitching in the postseason.

No problem. The usually pitching-rich Dodgers did not own the arms to shoot down the Redbirds in the NLDS. St. Louis won successive 8–3 games at Busch Stadium before polishing off its foe in four. But NLCS foe Houston boasted a terrific trio to stymie the best bats in baseball. Top two starters, Roy Oswalt and Roger Clemens (in the last of his seven Cy Young seasons at age forty-one), who had combined for a 38–14 record, and strikeout-machine closer Brad Lidge presented huge obstacles for the sizzling St. Louis hitters.

The Cardinals caught a break. Oswalt and Clemens were both unavailable in the first two games, having been needed to quell the Braves in the final two games of their first-round series. The Astros lacked depth in the rotation, and the Cardinals pounced. Pujols and soon-to-retire slugger Larry Walker, whom Jocketty had acquired in early August to bolster the lineup, battered Houston pitching at Busch Stadium to give their team a 2–0 lead before the teams headed to Minute Maid Park, where a collapse was imminent. Understandable defeats with Clemens and Oswalt followed, but it was eight innings of shutout ball by lightly regarded right-hander Brandon Backe and a rare meltdown by Isringhausen in Game 5 that placed St. Louis on the verge of elimination.

Game 6 unfolded into one of the most dramatic in MLB postseason history. An exhausted Isringhausen had maintained a 4–3 lead for 2.2 innings, and he needed one more out to force a Game 7. But he allowed an RBI single to future Hall of Famer Jeff Bagwell that eventually sent the battle into extra innings. That allowed Edmonds to play the role of hero. He destroyed a high fastball from Houston reliever Dan Miceli in the twelfth inning for the first walk-off home run in an NLCS game since 1986, setting off a raucous celebration on the field and in the crowd at Busch Stadium.

The task was far from complete. Another clash with Clemens awaited. An unfavorable matchup awaited, pitting Clemens against Jeff Suppan, who had been performing well in the playoffs but was still the team's fourth-best starter. But while the volatile superstar faltered in the sixth inning, allowing a two-run, tie-breaking homer by Rolen, his counterpart performed superbly after allowing a leadoff homer to Craig Biggio, shutting down the Astros through six with the help of a sensational diving catch by Edmonds in the second inning. The bullpen did the rest, and the Cardinals had won their first pennant in seventeen years.

Their first World Series triumph in nineteen years? That would be a whole new ball game. The Red Sox, seeking to break the eighty-six-year Curse of the Bambino, had just become the first team ever to overcome a 3–0 postseason deficit to win a series—and against the hated Yankees, no less. One could claim they arrived at the Fall Classic with more momentum and certainly greater inspiration than St. Louis. And those assertions could not be denied when Boston swept the Cardinals, who never recovered from a two-run, tiebreaking home run by Mark Bellhorn in the eighth inning of the opener that gave his team momentum it never relinquished.

The disappointing, lopsided defeat did little to subdue enthusiasm for Cardinals baseball. They had established a formula for success. They attracted three million fans a year. They spent smartly in free agency. They embraced continuity atop the organization with La Russa as manager and Jocketty as GM. They made wise trades that filled holes when necessary. Their farm system proved strong enough to replace retiring or fading veterans from the lineup and pitching staff. It was all working.

Among the rewards for their intelligence and patience was the health and fully blossoming of Carpenter, who, pain-free in 2005, finally arrived as the premier performer in the National League. He so impressed La Russa that the manager pegged him for the Opening Day assignment (and eventually the All-Star Game start, as well), in which he pitched well to beat Houston. The rejuvenated thirty-year-old took his momentum and ran with it to a 21–5 record, career-low 2.83 ERA and Cy Young Award.

Carpenter emerged as the ace of a previously starless rotation that keyed another one-hundred-win season despite the loss of their entire starting infield aside from Pujols. Jocketty continued to successfully replace those lost. Veteran shortstop Edgar Renteria left in free agency. No problem—Jocketty traded for diminutive dynamo David Eckstein. Fine second baseman Tony Womack signed elsewhere. No problem. Jocketty replaced him with veteran Mark Grudzielanek, who came through with a big year. Rolen injured his shoulder on a collision in June during a game against the Dodgers. Big problem. But offseason acquisition Abraham Nunez filled in admirably.

The expected offensive woes did not surface until after a three-game sweep of San Diego in the NLDS. And it was not the newcomers who struggled in the loss to Houston with the pennant hanging in the balance. Rather, it was veteran outfielders Walker, Edmonds, and Sanders, who had exploded for ten RBI in three games against the Padres. Astros stud hurlers Oswalt and an albeit fading Clemens simply outpitched their St. Louis counterparts.

The run of dominance appeared to have ended in 2006. Despite Rolen's return to health and production, only he and Pujols remained offensive forces. Brilliant young defensive catcher Yadier Molina, who would remain viable into his forties, had yet to hit his stride at the plate, and injuries had begun to take a toll on the thirty-six-year-old Edmonds. Free agent outfielder Juan Encarnacion managed one final hurrah in 2006 before ending his career the following year. And the rotation was a mess beyond Carpenter. Previously dependable Jason Marquis posted a disturbing 6.12 ERA and dubiously led the National League in runs and home runs allowed.

But the Redbirds were lucky. They competed in a terrible division. Hanging around .500 afforded them the luxury of remaining in contention. They even led the Central Division most of the year. The Cardinals seemed destined to cruise to the crown when they increased their lead to seven games with a defeat of Milwaukee on September 19. But they dropped four straight games to second-place Houston, then continued their collapse against San Diego and Houston at home. Their lead shrank to a half-game with only a series against Milwaukee at Busch Stadium remaining.

The big bats rose to the occasion. Pujols, Rolen, and Encarnacion battered Brewers pitching in a 10–5 victory while the Astros were falling to Atlanta. Then reserve slugger Scott Spiezio played the role of hero the following night by yanking a pinch-hit, bases-loaded triple down right-field line that turned a 2–0 deficit into a 3–2 lead in a division-clinching victory.

That the Cardinals backed into the playoffs motivated most experts to consider their appearance to be greatly ceremonial. They did not enter with momentum. Their hitting was little better than average. They featured no strong starting pitchers beyond Carpenter—a deadly reality in any baseball postseason. La Russa could only send such question marks as Jeff Weaver and Suppan to the mound against San Diego in the NLDS and hope for some strong innings and bullpen magic.

It worked beyond his wildest dreams. Carpenter was lights-out in the first game and clincher, which was made possible when Weaver shut out the Padres for five innings in Game 2. The Cardinals had pulled the first of three upsets in the 2006 postseason.

The unexpected strength of Weaver and Suppan continued in the NLCS against a powerful Mets lineup that featured one-hundred-RBI sluggers Carlos Delgado, David Wright, and Carlos Beltran. Suppan pitched eight shutout innings in Game 3, and Weaver won Game 5, to place their team on the precipice of the pennant. But when Carpenter lost Game 6 at Shea Stadium, with the decider scheduled the next night at the same venue, the club seemed destined to fall short. An epic pitchers' battle ensued, with Suppan on top of his game against southpaw Oliver Perez.

Ninth inning. Game tied at 1–1. The light-hitting Molina, who had batted .216 in the regular season, at the plate. One on, one out. Tough, young right-hander Aaron Heilman on the mound. Molina launched a towering blast over the left-field fence. Soon it was over. Rookie St. Louis right-hander Adam Wainwright polished the Mets off with his third save of the series, launching a wild celebration. "I don't think anyone expected, especially late in the season, that the St. Louis Cardinals would be in the World Series," Rolen crowed.[4]

The skeptics remained as they prepared to play the tough Tigers for the ultimate crown. Detroit had lost just once in the playoffs and featured an ace in right-handed Justin Verlander, who could pitch three times in a seven-game series. *USA Today* columnist Bob Nightengale jokingly predicted: "The Detroit Tigers' biggest obstacle to a championship will be keeping a straight face. The Tigers in three."[5]

Nightengale was right only about one team dominating. Rolen and Pujols set the tone by homering off Verlander early in the opener. The Tigers' roar had turned into a whimper. The Cardinals took the momentum after splitting the first two games in Detroit and ran with it to Busch Stadium. Carpenter dominated Game 3, an RBI double by eventual World Series MVP David Eckstein in the eighth inning won Game 4, then Weaver outdueled Verlander the next night to win it. Wainwright, who had taken over for the injured Isringhausen as closer, secured the championship by striking out Brandon Inge with the tying runs on base.

The unthinkable had happened. A team that barely finished over .500 in the regular season had captured the title. The 2006 Cardinals had laid claim to the distinction of "most unlikely champion in baseball history." The sellout throng at Busch cared nary a whit about any of that as they partied in the stands while their heroes celebrated on the field. "I'm looking around at all the confetti, and the fans are still here," exclaimed Wainwright, holding his month-old daughter in his arms. "This is such a great town and a great team. We fought so hard to be here. We deserve it, and they deserve it."[6]

St. Louis fans continued to deserve it as the twenty-first century gained steam. But their team would stumble a bit before regaining its stride.

CHAPTER TWENTY-ONE

One Hiccup, One Crown,
One Great Franchise

IT SEEMED THAT IF ANYONE IN BASEBALL HAD EARNED JOB SECURITY after one poor campaign, it was Cardinals general manager Walt Jocketty. His shrewd trades and the strengthening of the farm system had resulted in one winning season after another, as well as two pennants and one world championship in three years,

And if team owner Bill DeWitt had judged Jocketty only on victory and defeat, perhaps the latter would have remained in charge into the second decade of the twenty-first century. But DeWitt had other ideas before and after the club fell under .500 in 2007 for the first time since 1999. DeWitt had been bitten in 2003 by the analytics bug that gained favor in many front offices, and by the fame from the movie *Moneyball* about the success of the rebuilding in 2002 of Oakland Athletics. So, he surprised many around the sport by hiring businessman and data-driven Jeff Luhnow to run the scouting and player-development operations.

Though it lasted four years, the relationship between Luhnow and Jocketty remained strained. Both did their jobs well. Luhnow had played a huge role in the achievements of the minor league system, while Jocketty continued to add veteran pieces that kept the Cardinals flying high. Jocketty felt underappreciated and perceived that he was losing power within the organization. When DeWitt summoned Jocketty for a meeting four days after the conclusion of the 2007 season, he had no inkling that he was about to be handed a pink slip. The dismissal not only shocked Jocketty, who immediately accepted the GM job with Cincinnati, but it surprised and disappointed La Russa.

Luhnow remained in the same position. Youthful, new general manager John Mozeliak, who had been hired at the age of twenty-six as an assistant under Jocketty, tried to work better in concert with Luhnow. And it soon became obvious that the on-field struggles in 2007 were a hiccup rather than the start of a trend. The Redbirds began to win again.

Among the key contributors groomed on the farm was right-hander Adam Wainwright, who emerged as the ace in 2007, overcame a finger injury the following year to win eleven of fourteen decisions and lead the team in ERA again, then blossomed into one of the premier pitchers in the sport. He emerged as a strikeout pitcher in 2009 as his 19–8 record resulted in a third-place finish in the Cy Young Award balloting. The brilliance of Wainwright and the return from injury to greatness by Chris Carpenter keyed a run to the playoffs. It ended with a three-game sweep by the Dodgers, but the Cardinals had reestablished themselves as a title contender.

A trade engineered by Mozeliak that July strengthened the lineup and added a Robin to the Batman known as Albert Pujols. The Redbirds late that month acquired slugging outfielder Matt Holliday. Any fear that playing outside the rarefied air of Coors Field would weaken his numbers soon dissipated when Holliday batted .353 with thirteen home runs to help his new team win the division.

Holiday just kept on raking. He combined with Pujols for seventy home runs and 222 RBI in 2010, but the team simply lacked offensive depth beyond those two and started pitching aside from Wainwright and Carpenter to make the playoffs. And when it was announced in spring training 2011 that Wainwright would miss the entire year with an elbow injury, the notion of competing for a championship seemed rather far-fetched.

The skeptics underestimated what had for decades been the ability of the front office to piece together a contender, even if that required only temporary fixes. Among them in 2011 was thirty-five-year-old free agent Lance Berkman, the former Houston star who had one strong season left

Chris Carpenter rebounded from injuries to win the National League Cy Young Award for the Cardinals in 2005.

PHOTO COURTESY OF WIKIMEDIA COMMONS

Adam Wainwright was like Old Man River as he racked up one winning season after another for St. Louis.
PHOTO COURTESY OF WIKIMEDIA COMMONS

in him. Berkman batted .301 with thirty-one home runs and ninety-four RBI to help his new team lead the National League in runs scored.

The loss of Wainwright that left the Cardinals with a mediocre pitching staff never knocked them out of contention. Fellow starters such as Kyle Lohse and Jaime Garcia performed well enough to win with strong run support. St. Louis stayed in the division race most of the year before settling into a battle against Atlanta for the wild-card spot. They swept the Braves at Busch Stadium in mid-September before Carpenter blanked Houston in the final game of the regular season to clinch a place in the playoffs.

Carpenter was not done rising to the occasion. The powerful Phillies were expected to shoot down the Cardinals in the first round, but the underdogs battled the team that won 102 games into a do-or-die show-down in Philadelphia. The anticipated pitching duel between Carpenter and Phillies stud Roy Halladay materialized. St. Louis scored a run in the first, then the two standouts settled in to pitch nothing but shutout innings. Carpenter allowed no runners past first base after the fourth inning and finished with a three-hitter to catapult his team into the National League Championship Series against Milwaukee.

Some cited a loftier place in the standings and a sizzling finish to the regular season to predict a Brewer win. But premier pitchers most often dictate victory and defeat in the playoffs, and neither team boasted an ace. The Cardinals featured superior hitting, which took over the series. They pounded Milwaukee pitching, especially with the pennant on the line. After the Brewers won in St. Louis to knot the series at 2–2, the Redbirds scored nineteen runs on twenty-four hits in the last two games to bury their NL Central rival.

The unexpected offensive hero was emerging third baseman David Freese, who had lost two months early in the year to a broken hand after a torrid start. He batted an incredible .545 in the series, with three hom-ers and nine RBI. He finished with a flourish, slamming a homer and a double in his first two at-bats to set the tone for a St. Louis blowout—and for one of the most dramatic, incredible Fall Classics ever.

A mediocre Texas pitching staff shut down the Cardinals in four of the first five games. The lone exception was a sixteen-run explosion that featured a three-homer performance from Pujols—one of only four in World Series history. And when the Rangers headed into the eighth inning of Game 6 with a 7–4 lead, the sellout crowd at Busch Stadium sensed their team was doomed.

But the Redbirds responded with a series of comebacks that boggled the mind and cemented the name of Freese among the all-time post-season heroes. The infielder who would become little more than a solid

Third baseman David Freese played the role of World Series hero in 2011.
PHOTO COURTESY OF WIKIMEDIA COMMONS

starter came through time and again. He slammed an opposite-field, two-run triple with St. Louis one out from a series defeat to forge a tie. Troubled Texas slugger Josh Hamilton homered in the tenth to give his team a 9–7 lead. Soon the Cardinals were again on the brink of disaster, but a Berkman single knotted the score. Freese ended the drama by clobbering a home run to dead-center in the bottom of the eleventh as the delirious fans roared their approval to set up a Game 7 showdown. "If that's not the best postseason game of all time, I don't know what could top it," marveled Berkman. "That was unbelievable."[1]

St. Louis fans who anticipated a Rangers team, that a night earlier had twice been one out from a World Series victory, to play like a demoralized team were disappointed when they scored two runs off Carpenter in the first. But Freese (who else?) responded in the bottom of the inning with a two-run double that established the all-time postseason RBI record at twenty-one and sent the Cardinals soaring. Carpenter and his pitching mates tossed nothing but goose eggs the rest of the way, in a 6–2 victory that set off a wild celebration in St. Louis.

But the revelers had one disturbing thought in the back of their minds. And that was the impending free agency of Pujols. The club had made offers to keep the slugger in St. Louis, to no avail. They fell behind the Marlins and Angels in their bidding that offseason. The latter eventually lured him away with a ten-year, $254-million contract and milestone incentives. The final offer from St. Louis paled in comparison.

Speculation that the organization believed the thirty-two-year-old Pujols had begun the downside of his career was fueled by his 2011 numbers. His batting average fell under .300, and his RBI total dropped below one hundred for the first time in his career—though barely in both cases. Never mind that he finished second in the NL MVP voting after winning it the previous two seasons. Angels GM Jerry DiPoto wasn't complaining. "If you want to call 'decline' going from superhuman to great," he offered as a reply to the question of Pujols's production, "I don't think we've seen the last great days of Albert Pujols."[2] St. Louis GM John Mozeliak merely expressed satisfaction at the effort his team had made in trying to retain the superstar.

Nearly a decade of hindsight vindicated the Cardinals. Pujols continued his inevitable path to the Hall of Fame, but he never reached the level of production with Anaheim as he had with the Redbirds before returning to St. Louis for a final farewell in 2022. Though he added four one-hundred-RBI seasons, his batting average and on-base percentage fell precipitously, and he earned just one more All-Star Game appearance. And while the Angels watched the playoffs from home annually, the Cardinals continued to win consistently.

Mozeliak responded to the loss of Pujols by signing aging outfielder Carlos Beltran, who proved his bat remained potent by slamming fifty-six home runs over the next two years. The Cardinals replaced Pujols at first base temporarily with 2011 hero Allen Craig, whose productive postseason bat was overshadowed only by that of Freese.

All remained well offensively. But those bats no longer swung for the sixty-seven-year-old La Russa, who attended the championship parade in 2011 before announcing his retirement. He had informed the organization of his decision with the team foundering in August, but its comeback and title run changed nothing. The players expressed shock at his departure, but it was not one made in haste. "I think this just feels like the time to end it," said La Russa, who returned surprisingly at the age of seventy-six to manage the White Sox in 2021. "When I look in the mirror, I know I'd come back for the wrong reasons, and I didn't want to do that."[3]

The shock of his retirement was matched two weeks later by the hiring of former Cardinals catcher Mike Matheny as his replacement. Matheny had neither managed nor coached after retiring as a player in 2006, serving only with the club as a spring training advisor. That he beat out former Red Sox skipper Terry Francona for the job was even more stunning, given that the latter had broken the Curse of the Bambino and guided Boston to world championships in 2004 and 2007.

A new era of Redbirds baseball was about to begin. And the new manager proved himself worthy as a communicator and tactician from Day 1.

CHAPTER TWENTY-TWO

Often Close, Never a Cigar

THE HIRE OF INEXPERIENCED MIKE MATHENY AS CARDINALS MANAGER in 2012 was not without forethought. He had been a catcher in his playing days, after all, a position generally accepted as the best on-field training for his new job. Matheny had also gained a knowledge of the players' strengths and weaknesses while working with them in spring training.

He indeed earned a reputation as a keen tactician from the start. The Cardinals did not miss a beat after snagging the crown in 2011. The unexpected production of thirty-five-year-old Carlos Beltran and first baseman Allen Craig more than made up for the loss of free agent defector Albert Pujols, and the club even scored a few more runs than they had the previous year. The emergence of right-hander Lance Lynn, who won eighteen of twenty-five decisions, and the oddly late blossoming of veteran Kyle Lohse, whose .842 winning percentage led the National League, provided strong pitching depth. Matheny had plenty to work with in 2012.

What he did not have was the talent to compete with the cream of the NL crop. That included Central Division champion Cincinnati. But the Cardinals had good timing. Major League Baseball had instituted a one-game playoff round that season. The all-or-nothing wild card allowed them to remain in the postseason chase after falling hopelessly behind the Reds in early September. A 2–8 stretch that month placed them in a flatfooted tie with the Dodgers for the last spot. But a 12–4 finish not only set up a wild-card battle in Atlanta, but it gave them momentum.

The generous Braves committed three errors, one of which allowed three unearned runs to score in a 6–3 St. Louis victory. But the Cardinals appeared doomed when they fell behind Washington, 6–0, then 7–5 heading into the ninth inning of the deciding game of the division series. But they soon took advantage of the Nationals' fluid closer situation. Drew Storen had late in the year usurped Tyler Clippard in that role. He placed his team on the brink of an NLCS berth by retiring Matt Holliday and Craig after a Beltran double. But Storen walked Yadier Molina and David Freese to load the bases to bring weak-hitting second

Super catcher and fine hitter Yadier Molina was a fixture behind the plate for St. Louis during the second decade of the twenty-first century and beyond.

PHOTO COURTESY OF WIKIMEDIA COMMONS

baseman Daniel Descalso to the plate. Hope was not lost. Descalso, who had managed just four home runs during the regular season, had homered twice in the playoffs, including one in that game. He responded by bouncing a two-run single up the middle, forging a 9–9 tie. Then fellow middle infielder Pete Kozma, whose major league experience consisted of eighty-nine at-bats, ripped a single to right to drive in the winning runs and all but secure the largest comeback ever in a winner-take-all playoff game. The Redbirds were back in the NLCS.

Such heroics had grown commonplace. Fresh in the minds of baseball fans were the sterling Cardinal comebacks that resulted in a crown a year earlier. Matheny did not perceive it all as coincidental. "It's just the kind of people they are," he said in praising his players. "They believe in themselves. They believe in each other. . . . They just don't quit, and I think that says a lot about their character."[1]

They appeared destined to pass another test of character against the Giants with a pennant on the line. Fine pitching performances by Lohse and Wainwright placed them on a brink of a second consecutive World Series appearance. But inexplicably their arms faltered, and their bats went silent. The Cardinals were outscored 20–1 over the last three games as Lynn, Wainwright, and Lohse combined to pitching fewer than ten innings before knockout blows while their teammates managed just one hit in twenty-one at-bats with runners in scoring position. The clutch play that had defined their success had suddenly failed them.

It returned down the stretch in 2013. One reason was the sizzling bat of blossoming second baseman Matt Carpenter, who earned full-time status that season and finished fourth in the NL MVP voting after batting .318 and scoring 126 runs. Carpenter sizzled with the division title hanging in the balance, hitting safely in twenty-two of twenty-four games into late September as his team fought off Pittsburgh. The Cardinals swept a three-game series against the Pirates before 126,000 fans at Busch Stadium early that month to forge ahead and maintained their lead the rest of the way. They won their last six games to enter the first round against that same division rival on a tear.

Wainwright, who emerged that year as the undeniable ace of the staff, proved why against the Pirates. He beat them twice, allowing just one run both in the opener and critical Game 5 to vault the club into an NLCS showdown against Los Angeles. And in that series, another hurling hero emerged. That was twenty-two-year-old heralded rookie Michael Wacha, who joined the rotation after his promotion in late May and pitched brilliantly in September. The former first-round draft pick twice baffled the Dodgers in shutout performances, blanking them over seven innings in Game 6 to easily outduel ace Clayton Kershaw, who had that year won the third of four consecutive NL ERA titles.

His teammates were duly impressed. Among them was Beltran, who was nearly twice Wacha's age. "Since he joined the ballclub, all he has done is given us an opportunity to win ball games," Beltran said. "You guys are going to hear a lot from that kid, because that kid is very special. Being able to actually shut down an offense like the Dodgers . . . is unbelievable. The kid is a horse. He wants to be there. He loves the moment. It's great to watch a young kid be able to come through like that."[2]

Shoulder and oblique injuries prevented Wacha from reaching the lofty expectations predicted by Beltran, but he continued his mastery of opposing batters against Boston in Game 2 of the World Series as the Cardinals forged a tie. But after winning two nights later before a sellout crowd at Busch Stadium on a ninth-inning walk-off, they duplicated their offensive collapse of the 2012 NLCS. They scored just four runs over the last three games in falling to the Red Sox.

The following year proved most challenging to Matheny both on and off the field. He guided the team to another division crown despite a precipitous drop in offensive production from much of the lineup, including Molina, Craig, Carpenter, and Holiday. Only the continued brilliance of Wainwright and Lynn, as well as dependable flame-throwing closer Trevor Rosenthal, prevented disaster. A sweep of second-place Pittsburgh before packed houses at home to start September pushed the Cardinals into a first-place standing they never relinquished.

The Dodgers arrived for the NLDS seeking revenge, but they never earned the satisfaction. An eight-run seventh inning capped by a Holiday three-run homer handed St. Louis the opener, and another three-run blast by power-hitting first baseman Matt Adams in Game 4 all but wiped out Los Angeles. But Redbird weaknesses proved too deep to overcome in

Mike Matheny played for the Cardinals before managing them to an NL title in 2013.
PHOTO COURTESY OF WIKIMEDIA COMMONS

the NLCS against San Francisco, which ended when journeyman Travis Ishikawa slugged a three-run homer in the ninth inning of Game 5.

The challenge Matheny faced managing an underperforming offensive team into the playoffs paled in comparison to the one that arose on October 26, when popular and promising Cardinals outfielder Oscar Taveras was killed in a car accident in his native Dominican Republic. Matheny had fostered a father-son relationship with the twenty-two-year-old Taveras, whom he criticized publicly in the name of tough love for what he perceived as a poor work ethic and lack of focus. Now it was time for Matheny to turn tragedy into a strengthening of family. He wrote the following message in the wake of Taveras's death, which he hoped would bring all the Cardinals together as one:

> *In my opinion, the word "ove" is the most misused, and misunderstood word in the English language. It is not popular for men to use this word, and even less popular for athletes. But there is not a more accurate word for how a group of men share a deep and genuine concern for each other. We loved Oscar, and he loved us. That is what a team does, that is what a family does. You will be missed, Oscar.*[3]

Those who considered Matheny a miracle worker in 2014 cemented that belief the next season, when he guided another band of no-hit

185

wonders to a one-hundred-win season. Cardinals general manager John Mozeliak all but stood pat in the offseason in the belief the previous track records of those who struggled promised rebounds. His only significant move to bolster the attack was signing fading free agent first baseman and strikeout machine Mark Reynolds, who batted .230 and provided far less power than hoped. His meager output and injuries that signaled the beginning of the end for Holliday's career resulted in the Redbirds struggling mightily to score.

Yet despite their meager output, the Cardinals soared. They snagged first place in the Central Division in mid-April and never let go. Their primary strength was pitching depth despite the loss of Wainwright to injury. Promising young starter Carlos Martinez, who failed years later to maximize his potential, and bounce-back southpaw Jaime Garcia joined veteran offseason trade acquisition John Lackey, Lynn, and Wacha to form a dynamite quintet. And with Rosenthal peaking in a forty-eight-save season, the pitchers gave their team a chance to win nearly every night.

The Matheny magic disappeared, however, in the first round of the playoffs against division rival Chicago. So did the lights-out arms after Lackey, super setup man Kevin Siegrist, and Rosenthal combined to blank the Cubs in the opener. Neither Garcia, nor Wacha, nor Lackey survived past the fifth inning over the next three games. Even Siegrist faltered in Game 5, turning a 4–4 tie into a 6–4 defeat that forced the Cardinals into an earlier-than-wanted vacation.

That would prove disappointingly to be the last playoff run of the Matheny era. The Cardinals remained strong through 2018, but he was fired in mid-July that season and replaced by bench coach Mike Shildt. The 2016 team tried uncharacteristically to bash its way to victory during a baseball era that accentuated power, even leading the National League in home runs. It scored 132 more runs than the 2015 club, yet it lost fourteen more games, partly because of the downfall of Rosenthal, who lost his control and his job in late June before hitting the disabled list with a shoulder injury.

A late collapse in 2017 and fall from contention in the summer of 2018 cost Matheny his job. Among the reasons cited for his departure was a strained relationship with outfielder Dexter Fowler, who had in 2017 signed a free-agent contract for $16.5 million per season. Fowler barely performed to expectations that year but fell apart in 2018. He was batting just .174 in mid-July after Matheny publicly questioned his "effort and energy level."[4]

The Cardinals slapped the interim tag on Shildt, but a 22–6 blitz in August that vaulted the team into contention bought him another year. And Shildt took full advantage. Ownership helped by signing premier free-agent slugger Paul Goldschmidt to fill what had been a gaping hole

First baseman Paul Goldschmidt arrived from Arizona and remained one of the top hitters in baseball.

PHOTO COURTESY OF WIKIMEDIA COMMONS

at first base. Promising right-hander Jack Flaherty, whose shoulder problems limited him in later years, emerged as an ace, finishing fourth in the Cy Young Award voting.

The result was a yo-yo season, during which the Redbirds fell under .500 in mid-July, embarked on a tear that vaulted them into first place, lost all five games on a road trip against the Athletics and Dodgers to fall back again, sizzled into late September, then collapsed again. They needed a win before a sellout crowd at Busch on the final day of the regular season to win the division. And thanks to Flaherty, who pitched shutout ball, and home runs in consecutive innings by Fowler, Carpenter, and Goldschmidt, the Cardinals made a playoff date with Atlanta.

Catcher Yadier Molina, whose fine hitting had always been overshadowed by his defensive brilliance, played hero with his bat against the Braves with his team on the verge of defeat in Game 4. His eighth-inning single tied it, and his sacrifice fly in the tenth won it. That gave Flaherty another opportunity to shine in the spotlight. The offense allowed him to cruise, sending Braves fans to the exits early and killing all the drama with a ten-run first inning.

The Redbirds were not destined for such explosions against NLCS foe Washington. The Nationals, after all, featured two of the finest pitchers in the sport in Max Scherzer and Stephen Strasburg, who had led the National League with eighteen wins. It seemed St. Louis had caught a break when neither was available for the opener and lesser-light Anibal Sanchez took the mound instead. But the Cardinals managed just one hit against Sanchez and closer Sean Doolitle, setting the tone for a disastrous series. They scored just two runs on ten hits against Scherzer, Strasburg, and the Washington bullpen over the next two games combined, then St. Louis starter Dakota Hudson allowed seven runs in the first inning of Game 4 to the eventual World Series champions.

The Cardinals had batted a shocking .130 in the sweep. Fowler went hitless in eleven at-bats before being benched by Shildt. Goldschmidt and cleanup hitter Marcell Ozuna struck out in ten consecutive at-bats at one point. The former managed just one hit in the series. "There's not one thing you can point to," said Goldschmidt about the unlikely sweep.

"One hit in four games, that's not going to cut it when you're hitting third. It just came back to bite us."[5]

Mozeliak continued to spend big bucks so his team would not be bitten again. After a season limited to sixty games by the COVID-19 pandemic, he traded for super Colorado slugger and brilliant third baseman Nolan Arenado, taking on his $35-million annual contract. The deal came with one major risk: What if Arenado could not match his production with the Rockies, who played their home games in the rarefied air of Coors Field? But though Arenado did lose some power at Busch, he led the 2021 Cardinals in home runs and RBI. Arenado, Goldschmidt, and emerging outfielder Tyler O'Neill formed a deadly trio, but the Cardinals lacked depth in their lineup and in their rotation beyond Wainwright. A defeat to the Dodgers in the wild-card game ended their season and sealed the fate of Shildt. His Cardinals had set a team record by winning seventeen straight in September to turn a lost season into a postseason berth, but he was fired in favor of thirty-five-year-old bench coach Oliver Marmol.

"I have a broken heart" Shildt said months later, after being told he was let go for what the organization described as "philosophical differences." "It still hurts. It hurts bad. When it first happened, I broke down. I was inconsolable."[6]

Time marched on. It did not seem to matter who managed the Redbirds—they would remain a winner. As Marmol prepared to take over the club, they had not suffered through a losing season since 2007. They had reached the postseason in fifteen of the previous twenty-two years. That the Cardinals would soar was a given. The only question was how high. Arguably, the most passionate fan base in America could hardly wait each spring to find out.

NOTES

Chapter 1

1. Mike Eisenbath, *The Cardinals Encyclopedia* (Philadelphia: Temple University Press, 1999), 8, https://books.google.com/books?id=hymGG28xYcoC&pg=PA8&lpg =PA8&dq=St.+Louis+Brown+Stockings+Lip+Pike&source=bl&ots=uQ9E-B62eJ &sig=ACfU3U23vNSW1sUqjqnCGOWmyPqsbsIqGg&hl=en&sa=X&ved=2ahUKE wid67mSgsP1AhVsLTQIHRTVDUMQ6AF6BAgUEAM#v=onepage&q=St.%20 Louis%20Brown%20Stockings%20Lip%20Pike&f=false.

2. Jon David Cash, *Before They Were Cardinals: Major League Baseball in Nineteenth Century St. Louis* (Columbia, MO: University of Missouri Press, 2002), 34. https:// books.google.com/books?id=xDKzBhhDcZEC&pg=PA33&lpg=PA33&dq=1876 +Championship+of+the+West:+Brown+Stockings&source=bl&ots=Ej8UkEHGx7&sig =ACfU3U1ZBBOqVYyHchLy1vzNGuwqAOQpWg&hl=en&sa=X&ved=2ahUKEwj dhsKqisP1AhX-JzQIHbB5AWkQ6AF6BAgvEAM#v=onepage&q=1876%20Cham pionship%20of%20the%20West%3A%20Brown%20Stockings&f=false.

3. Mike Bates, "Chris von der Ahe, and the terrible, awful, no good, very bad year," *Hardball Times*, February 16, 2018, https://tht.fangraphs.com/chris-von-der-ahe-and -the-terrible-awful-no-good-very-bad-year/.

Chapter 3

1. Mark Rothenberg, "A telegram that changed baseball history," National Baseball Hall of Fame, https://baseballhall.org/discover/short-stops/a-telegram-that-changed -baseball-history.

2. Joan M. Thomas, "Roger Bresnahan," Society for American Baseball Research, https://sabr.org/bioproj/person/roger-bresnahan/.

3. Ibid.

Chapter 4

1. Todd Radom, "The Cardinals' 'bird-on-the-bat' logo opened to mixed reviews in 1922," April 7, 2015, https://www.toddradom.com/blog/the-cardinals-birds-on-bat-logo -opened-to-mixed-reviews-in-1922.

2. Dick Farrington, "Branch Rickey, Defending Farms, Says Stark Necessity Forced System," *Sporting News,* December 1, 1932, 3.

Chapter 5

1. Charles C. Alexander, *Rogers Hornsby: A Biography* (New York: Henry Holt & Co., 1995), https://books.google.com/books?id=MWH1AAAAQBAJ&pg=PT52&lpg=PT52&dq=Mary+Rogers+Hornsby+charles+c.+alexander+Fort+Worth&source=bl&ots=d13WJcfnBZ&sig=ACfU3U3Eb0QZmJ9vQckUCmvmJR1EODbUDw&hl=en&sa=X&ved=2ahUKEwjp8Ojgx5H2AhU_FTQIHXDBCygQ6AF6BAg0EAM#v=onepage&q=Mary%20Rogers%20Hornsby%20charles%20c.%20alexander%20Fort%20Worth&f=false.
2. Ibid.
3. Jonathan D'Amore, *Rogers Hornsby, A Biography* (Boston: Greenwood Publishing, 2004), 37.
4. Larry Schwartz, "Hornsby cared only about results," ESPN.com, http://www.espn.com/sportscentury/features/00014249.html.
5. Anthony J. Connor, *Voices from Cooperstown: Baseball's Hall of Famers Tell It Like It Was* (New York: Macmillan Publishing Company, 1984).
6. Red Barber, "Baseball's Frisch-for-Hornsby as big as any player trade ever," *Christian Science Monitor*, August 26, 1988, https://www.csmonitor.com/1988/0826/ptrade.html.
7. Janey Murray, "Blockbuster trade sends Hornsby to Giants, Frisch to Cardinals," National Baseball Hall of Fame, https://baseballhall.org/discover/inside-pitch/blockbuster-trade-sends-hornsby-to-giants-frisch-to-cardinals.

Chapter 6

1. Craig Muder, "Alexander provides ultimate relief for Cardinals in 1926 World Series," National Baseball Hall of Fame, https://baseballhall.org/discover/inside-pitch/alexander-1926-world-series.
2. Gary Livacari, "The Classic 1926 World Series: 'Ol Pete' Alexander comes to the rescue," Baseball History Comes Alive, October 17, 2020, https://www.baseballhistorycomesalive.com/the-classic-1926-world-series-ol-pete-alexander-comes-to-the-rescue/.

Chapter 7

1. *Golden Baseball Magazine* staff, "1931—Game 7: Philadelphia Athletics @ St. Louis Cardinals," *Golden Baseball Magazine*, http://goldenrankings.com/ultimategame1931.html.
2. LE, "MLB—1934—ESPN Baseball's Greatest Hits special feature—the St. Louis Cardinals Gas House Gang," Imasportsphile, February 9, 2019, https://imasportsphile.com/mlb-1934-espn-baseballs-greatest-hits-special-feature-the-st-louis-cardinals-gas-house-gang/.
3. Gary Livacari, "1934 World Series and the 'Gas House Gang': Baseball History Comes Alive," March 7, 2016, https://www.baseballhistorycomesalive.com/1934-world-series-and-the-gas-house-gang/.
4. Joseph Wancho, "Dizzy Dean," Society for American Baseball Research, https://sabr.org/bioproj/person/dizzy-dean/.
5. Scott Ferkovich, "Tigers lost hotly contested battle with Cardinals in 1934 World Series," Vintage Detroit, May 29, 2017, https://www.vintagedetroit.com/tigers-lost-hotly-contested-battle-cardinals-1934-world-series/.

6. Joseph Wancho, "Dizzy Dean," Society for American Baseball Research, https://sabr.org/bioproj/person/dizzy-dean/.

7. Carl Duncan, *Me 'N' Paul: The Legend of Dizzy and Daffy* (Bloomington, IN: iUniverse, 2020), https://books.google.com/books?id=C70OEAAAQBAJ&pg=PT278&lpg=PT278&dq=jimmie+wilson:+%E2%80%9CIt%E2%80%99s+getting+so+you+can%E2%80%99t+get+a+base+hit+off+those+Deans+without+getting+beaned+your+next+time+up.+They+think+they+can+get+away+with+anything,+but+by+God,+the+Phils+have+declared+war+on+them.%E2%80%9D&source=bl&ots=LAAS7xLaKW&sig=ACfU3U2UCSO2sWljIeiaWPOPCBrLBXf3qg&hl=en&sa=X&ved=2ahUKEwjKs4jyq772AhUJLTQIHaygD_cQ6AF6BAgCEAM#v=onepage&q=jimmie%20wilson%3A%20%E2%80%9CIt%E2%80%99s%20getting%20so%20you%20can%E2%80%99t%20get%20a%20base%20hit%20off%20those%20Deans%20without%20getting%20beaned%20your%20next%20time%20up.%20They%20think%20they%20can%20get%20away%20with%20anything%2C%20but%20by%20God%2C%20the%20Phils%20have%20declared%20war%20on%20them.%E2%80%9D&f=false.

8. Robert Gregory, *Diz: The Story of Dizzy Dean and Baseball During the Great Depression* (New York: Viking, 1992).

Chapter 8

1. "A Hundred Grand Orgy," *Sporting News,* May 16, 1935, 5.

2. Retrosimba, "Rift with Branch Rickey led Cards to oust Frankie Frisch," September 9, 2013, https://retrosimba.com/2013/09/09/rift-with-branch-rickey-led-cards-to-oust-frankie-frisch/.

3. Ibid.

Chapter 9

1. Bill Francis, "All-St. Louis World Series brought out the best in Cardinals, Browns," Baseball Hall of Fame, https://baseballhall.org/discover/all-st-louis-world-series-brought-out-the-best-in-cardinals-browns.

2. Matt Kelly, "Cardinals, Dodgers face off in baseball's first three-game playoff," Baseball Hall of Fame, https://baseballhall.org/discover/inside-pitch/1946-nl-playoff.

3. Baseball Almanac, "1946 World Series," https://www.baseball-almanac.com/ws/yr1946ws.shtml.

4. Warren Corbett, "Eddie Dyer," Society for American Baseball Research, https://sabr.org/bioproj/person/eddie-dyer/.

5. *Time* staff, "Sport: Sam's last sale," *Time,* December 8, 1947, http://content.time.com/time/subscriber/article/0,33009,934146,00.html.

Chapter 10

1. Larry Schwartz, "Musial was gentleman killer," ESPN Classic, http://www.espn.com/classic/biography/s/Musial_Stan.html.

2. Anne Rogers, "How Cards' legend Stan Musial became 'The Man,'" MLB.com, November 19, 2020, https://www.mlb.com/news/stan-musial-the-man-nickname-origin#:~:text=In%201946%2C%20Musial%20earned%20the,St.

3. Historic Missourians staff, "Stan Musial," *Historic Missourians*, https://historic missourians.shsmo.org/stan-musial.

4. Gary Livacari, "The beginning—the crises—the third MVP," *Baseball History Comes Alive*, March 9, 2021, https://www.baseballhistorycomesalive.com/stan-musial-the-be ginning-the-crises-the-third-mvp/.

5. Ibid.

6. Jan Finkel, "Stan Musal," Society for American Baseball Research, https://sabr.org /bioproj/person/stan-musial/.

7. Larry Schwartz, "Musial was gentleman killer," ESPN Classic, http://www.espn .com/classic/biography/s/Musial_Stan.html.

8. Greg Botelho, "Baseball great Stan 'The Man' Musial dies at 92," CNN, March 7, 2013, https://www.cnn.com/2013/01/19/sport/missouri-musial-obit/index.html.

Chapter 11

1. John C. Skipper, *A Biographical Dictionary of Major League Baseball Managers* (Jefferson, NC: McFarland, 2003).

2. Retrosimba, "Frank Lane and his tumultuous stint as Cardinals GM," October 8, 2015, https://retrosimba.com/2015/10/08/frank-lane-and-his-tumultuous-stint-as-car dinals-gm/.

3. Ibid.

4. *Time* staff, "Sport: Relaxed Redbird," *Time*, June 13, 1955, http://content.time.com /time/subscriber/article/0,33009,861539,00.html.

5. Clay Eals, "Fred Hutchinson," Society for American Baseball Research, https://sabr .org/bioproj/person/fred-hutchinson/.

6. Ibid.

Chapter 12

1. Peter Golenbock, *The Spirit of St. Louis* (New York: Harper & Brothers, 2000), 423.

2. Warren Corbett, "Solly Hemus," Society for American Baseball Research, https:// sabr.org/bioproj/person/solly-hemus/.

3. Bing Devine, *The Memoirs of Bing Devine: Stealing Lou Brock and Other Brilliant Moves by a Master G.M.* (Sports Publishing, 2004), 112.

4. Alex Coffey, "Lou Brock traded to Cardinals," Baseball Hall of Fame, https://base ballhall.org/discover-more/stories/inside-pitch/lou-brock-traded-to-cards.

5. Ibid.

6. Ibid.

7. Ibid.

8. Matt Kelly, "Bob Gibson wills Cardinals to Game 7 victory in 1964 World Series," Baseball Hall of Fame, https://baseballhall.org/discover-more/stories/inside-pitch/gib son-cardinals-victory-1964-world-series.

9. Retrosimba, "Why Bob Gibson finished the 1964 World Series," November 4, 2015, https://retrosimba.com/2015/11/04/bob-gibson-matt-harvey-and-world-series-ninths/.

10. Bob Gibson with Lonnie Wheeler, *Stranger to the Game: The Autobiography of Bob Gibson* (New York: Penguin Books, 1994), 82–83.

Chapter 13

1. Ibid., 52–53.

2. Ibid., 10–11.

3. Terry Sloope, "Bob Gibson," Society for American Baseball Research, https://sabr.org/bioproj/person/bob-gibson/.

4. Bob Gibson with Lonnie Wheeler, *Stranger to The Game: The Autobiography of Bob Gibson* (New York: Penguin Books, 1994), 62.

5. Craig Murder, "Gibson completes fantastic 1968 season with NL MVP honors," Baseball Hall of Fame, https://baseballhall.org/discover/inside-pitch/gibson-completes-fantastic-1968-season-with-nl-mvp-honors.

6. Derek Cofelt, "Righting a wrong: Why Bob Gibson deserves more respect from baseball writers," *Bleacher Report*, January 16, 2009, https://bleacherreport.com/articles/111849-righting-a-wrong-why-bob-gibson-deserves-more-respect-from-baseball-writers.

7. Joe Trimble, "Dazed Denny on Gibson: 'Greatest I've ever seen'," *New York Daily News*, October 3, 1968, 117.

8. Bob Gibson with Lonnie Wheeler, *Stranger to the Game: The Autobiography of Bob Gibson* (New York: Penguin Books, 1994).

Chapter 14

1. Mike Mandel, *San Francisco Giants: An Oral History*, 1979, 155.

2. Greg Erion, "May 8, 1966: Cardinal's play their last game at Sportsman's Park," Society for American Baseball Research, https://sabr.org/gamesproj/game/may-8-1966-cardinals-play-their-last-game-at-sportsmans-park/.

3. William Leggett, "Aftermath of a bittersweet World Series," *Sports Illustrated*, October 23, 1967, https://vault.si.com/vault/1967/10/23/aftermath-of-a-bittersweet-world-series.

4. Ibid.

5. Retrosimba, "Should Curt Flood have caught Jim Northrup's drive?" June 12, 2011, https://retrosimba.com/2011/06/12/should-curt-flood-have-caught-jim-northrups-drive/.

Chapter 15

1. Curt Flood, *The Way It Is* (Trident Press, 1971), 145–51.

2. Ibid., 158.

3. Retrosmba, "Gussie Busch vs. Steve Carlton: Hard heads play hardball," March 9, 2020, https://retrosimba.com/2020/03/09/gussie-busch-vs-steve-carlton-hard-heads-play-hardball/.

4. Parton Keese, "St. Louis loses to 3-run clout," *New York Times*, October 2, 1974, https://www.nytimes.com/1974/10/02/archives/st-louis-loses-to-2run-clout.html.

5. Retrosimba, "The day the Cardinals fired Red Schoendienst," October 5, 2016, https://retrosimba.com/2016/10/05/the-day-the-cardinals-fired-red-schoendienst/.

6. History of the Cardinals, "Rapp, Vern—Cardinals manager, 1977–1978," https://www.historyofcardinals.com/rapp-vern-cardinals-manager/.

7. Retrosimba, "Why Gussie Busch fired Bing Devine a second time," October 17, 2018, https://retrosimba.com/2018/10/17/why-gussie-busch-fired-bing-devine-a-second-time/.

Chapter 16

1. Dan O'Neill, "Aug. 26, 1981: Garry Templeton's Ladies' Day eruption," *St. Louis Post-Dispatch*, August 26, 2021, https://www.stltoday.com/sports/baseball/professional /aug-26-1981-garry-templetons-ladies-day-eruption/article_e2ebeb70-ce60-592f-a506 -99c938347842.html.

2. Joe Trezza, "Remembering the Cards' magical 1982 title," MLB.com, January 7, 2022, https://www.mlb.com/news/remembering-cardinals-1982-world-series.

3. YouTube, "1982 World Series, Game 7: Brewers at Cardinals," https://www.you tube.com/watch?v=veJj5iI4TM8&ab_channel=MLBVault.

4. Ibid.

5. YouTube, "1985 NLCS Gm5: Ozzie Smith's walk-off homer wins Game 5," https:// www.youtube.com/watch?v=L4PB0XoLbm8&ab_channel=MLB.

6. Ron Cervenka, "The (almost) forgotten devastating home run against the Dodgers," Think Blue, March 25, 2020, https://thinkbluela.com/2020/03/the-almost-forgotten -devastating-home-run-against-the-dodgers/.

7. Frederick C. Bush. "October 26, 1985: Royals force Game 7 after Cardinals' collapse in wake of Denkinger's call," Society for American Baseball Research, https://sabr .org/gamesproj/game/october-26-1985-royals-force-game-7-after-cardinals-collapse-in -wake-of-denkingers-call/.

Chapter 17

1. Retrosimba, "Jose Oquendo packed potent pennant punch for Cards," October 14, 2017, https://retrosimba.com/2017/10/14/jose-oquendo-packed-potent-pennant -punch-for-cards/.

2. Rick Hummel, "On July 6, 1990: Whitey Herzog quits as Cardinals manager," *St. Louis Post-Dispatch*, July 6, 2021, https://www.stltoday.com/sports/baseball/pro fessional/cardinal-beat/on-july-6-1990-whitey-herzog-quits-as-cardinals-manager/arti cle_e3f8171f-e270-57f9-9e58-c3ec864b1bd5.html#:~:text=Editor's%20note%3A%20 When%20Whitey%20Herzog,edition%20of%20the%20Post%2DDispatch.

3. Stew Thornley, "Walt Jocketty," Society for American Baseball Research, https:// sabr.org/bioproj/person/walt-jocketty/.

Chapter 18

1. Richard Justice, "McGwire surpasses Maris with 62nd home run," *Washington Post*, September 8, 1998, https://www.washingtonpost.com/wp-srv/sports/baseball/longterm /chase/articles/mac9.htm.

2. Jayson Stark, "Ankiel's October torture chamber strikes again," ESPN, October 13, 2000, https://www.espn.com/mlb/playoffs2000/2000/1012/814972.html.

Chapter 19

1. Ballparking It, "Busch Stadium: It's nice to #StayHome," stay home, April 9, 2020, https://ballparkingit.com/.

2. Staci D. Kramer, "Love affair continues in St. Louis," *Christian Science Monitor*, October 26, 2004, https://vindyarchives.com/news/2004/oct/26/love-affair-continues -in-st-louis/.

3. Retrosimba, "How Dizzy Dean became a baseball broadcaster," July 10, 2021, https://retrosimba.com/2021/07/10/how-dizzy-dean-became-a-baseball-broadcaster/.

4. Jack Buck, with Rob Rains and Bob Broeg, *That's a Winner!* (Champaign, IL: Sagamore Publishing, 1999).

5. Retrosimba, "Mike Shannon thought Cards broadcast job might last a year," January 25, 2014, https://retrosimba.com/2014/01/15/mike-shannon-thought-cards-broadcast -job-might-last-a-year/.

6. Ibid.

7. Lil Scooter. "Everyone has a favorite Mike 'Shannonism'—A hunt and peck," *SB Nation*, June 21, 2016, https://www.vivaelbirdos.com/st-louis-cardinals-news-anal ysis-mlb/2016/6/21/11989016/everyone-has-a-favorite-mike-shannonism-a-hunt -and-peck.

8. Joe Buck, "Guideposts Classics: Joe Buck on his hero, his father," *Guideposts*, https:// www.guideposts.org/friends-and-family/family/guideposts-classics-joe-buck-on-his -hero-his-father.

Chapter 20

1. STLRedbirds.com, "November 12, 2001: Albert Pujols is unanimous Rookie of the Year selection," October 9, 2021, https://www.stlredbirds.com/2021/10/09/albert-pujols -is-unanimous-rookie-of-the-year-selection/.

2. Ibid.

3. Jack Dougherty, "The tragic death of Cardinals pitcher Darryl Kile stunned the baseball world," *Sportscasting*, June 24, 2020, https://www.sportscasting.com/the-tragic -death-of-cardinals-pitcher-darryl-kile-stunned-the-baseball-world/.

4. Mike Fitzpatrick, "Cardinals beat Mets to win NL pennant," *Associated Press*, October 20, 2006, https://www.heraldtribune.com/story/news/2006/10/20/cardinals-beat -mets-to-win-nl-pennant/28507498007/.

5. Jonah Birenbaum, "The 2006 Cardinals had no business winning it all, but they did," *The Score*, https://www.thescore.com/mlb/news/1972066.

6. Tyler Kepner, "Cardinals paint crown red," *New York Times*, October 28, 2006, https://www.nytimes.com/2006/10/28/sports/baseball/28series.html.

Chapter 21

1. Joe Strauss, "Comeback special," *St. Louis Post-Dispatch*, October 28, 2011,

2. Joe Strauss, "Pujols signs with Angels: 10 years, $254 million," *St. Louis Post-Dispatch*, December 8, 2011, https://www.stltoday.com/sports/baseball/professional/pujols-signs -with-angels-10-years-254-million/article_9181b070-21ae-11e1-93ef-0019bb30f31a .html.

3. *ESPN* staff, "Tony La Russa announces retirement," *ESPN*, October 31, 2011, https:// www.espn.com/mlb/story/_/id/7173381/tony-la-russa-st-louis-cardinals-says-retiring.

Chapter 22

1. *Associated Press* staff, "Cardinals score 4 in 9th to stun Nationals, return to NLCS," *Associated Press*, October 12, 2012, https://www.espn.com/mlb/recap?gameId=321012120.

2. Adam McCalvy, "Wacha! Wacha! No joke, rookie named NLCS MVP," MLB. com, October 19, 2013, https://www.mlb.com/cardinals/news/st-louis-cardinals-rookie -michael-wacha-named-nlcs-mvp/c-63123156.

3. Bernie Miklasz, "Bernie: Matheny is right; Cards are family," *St. Louis Post-Dispatch*, October 30, 2014, https://www.stltoday.com/sports/baseball/professional/bernie-matheny -is-right-cards-are-family/article_01e5ac2e-7251-54d3-95e9-eff2025d8f31.html.

4. *ESPN* staff, "Cardinals fire manager Mike Matheny; bench coach Mike Shildt to serve in interim," *ESPN*, July 14, 2018, https://www.espn.com/mlb/story/_/id/24100246 /mike-matheny-fired-st-louis-cardinals-manager.

5. Stephen Whyno, "Cardinals implode in 1st inning, swept by Nationals in NLCS," *AP News*, October 16, 2019, https://apnews.com/article/mlb-sports-baseball-washing ton-nationals-st-louis-cardinals-83f4546bd7d44cbb858876e5f828ea80.

6. Steven Taranto, "Ex-Cardinals manager Mike Shildt says he has 'broken heart' after firing by St. Louis," *CBS Sports*, April 1, 2022, https://www.cbssports.com/mlb/news /ex-cardinals-manager-mike-shildt-says-he-has-broken-heart-after-firing-by-st-louis/.